HEADLINES AND DEADLINES

HEADLINES AND DEADLINES

A MANUAL FOR COPY EDITORS

by ROBERT E. GARST
Assistant Managing Editor, The New York Times

and THEODORE M. BERNSTEIN
Assistant Managing Editor, The New York Times

Third Edition
New York and London
COLUMBIA UNIVERSITY PRESS

Third Edition 1961
Third printing and Columbia Paperback edition 1963

Manufactured in the United States of America

FOREWORD

IN HIS FOREWORD to the first edition of *Headlines and Deadlines* my distinguished predecessor, Dean Carl W. Ackerman, wrote that although journalism may never become an exact science it should become a more exacting profession.

Evidence of this trend is to be found in the much higher educational level of today's newspapermen over those of a generation or two ago, in the rapidly increasing literature of journalism, and in the more adult and perceptive handling of the news in the better American newspapers. Further important evidence lies in the fact that a third edition (and sixth printing) of this extraordinarily useful little volume is called for today. The new edition recognizes and emphasizes the current progress in news writing, directed at making the news more understandable through the addition of background and perspective.

Like the earlier editions, this one is primarily a manual for the copy editor, who is gaining in importance as the profession grows more exacting. At the same time, *Headlines and Deadlines* is of such value to anyone in the profession that it is one of the basic books assigned to every student in the Graduate School of Journalism at Columbia.

Both of the authors are graduates of that school; both distinguished themselves for many years as members of its faculty; and both have played important roles in the continued progress of one of the truly great newspapers of all time. Between them, they possess rare qualifications in news judgment, in knowledge of editorial management, in teaching aptitude and in the effective use of the English language.

Through teaching and writing, the team of Garst and Bernstein already has had appreciable effect on the new generation of journalistic leadership. Through this new edition, I hope, it will have more.

EDWARD W. BARRETT

November, 1960
Graduate School of Journalism
Columbia University

PREFACE

COPY EDITING is one field in which the demand for workers usually exceeds the supply. This is likely to be permanently so because in an ideal sense there never will be a copy editor who knows enough to fill the requirements of his job thoroughly. The ideal copy editor not only would have a complete mastery over the technical phases of his work, such as the editing of copy and the writing of headlines, but would possess sound and swift judgment, would be an expert rhetorician and grammarian and would be thoroughly versed in government, politics, astrophysics, home gardening, shoes, ships, sealing wax and all subjects that find or are likely to find a place in the kaleidoscopic enterprise that is the modern newspaper.

Obviously, then, no book can furnish all the equipment that the copy editor is expected to bring to his work. A book cannot instill judgment; it cannot supply a broad mental background, which after all, is cumulative. But what it can do is to explain the technique of copy editing. That is the aim of the present volume.

What the authors have sought to do is to set before journalists—practicing, as well as aspiring—the best standards of the metropolitan press. This involves no reflection on rural journalism, for the two are not things apart; rural practice is, rather, an adaptation of metropolitan practice to the more personal and informal needs of the small-town newspaper.

While, from the point of view of the rural press, the standards presented may be too rigid, from the point of view of the individual newspaperman they are indispensable if he wishes to follow his profession into whatever field it may beckon him. The journalist trained for rural practice alone would be dismayed if suddenly he found himself on a city daily. On the other hand, the journalist equipped with metropolitan standards could adapt himself almost immediately to rural technical requirements.

Hence, what this book seeks to do is not to reform journalism, but to train journalists. Its purpose is to give so thorough and basic instruction that the copy editor will be able to make his way on the desk of a newspaper anywhere.

The copy editor's work falls naturally into two main divisions: editing copy and writing headlines. This book is, therefore, similarly divided. Included in the section on editing is a condensed list of "Abused Words" which calls attention to the more common errors made in newspapers. Appended to the section on headlines is a "Headline Vocabulary of Related Words" in which the words are grouped by their meanings under key words listed alphabetically. This list, which should prove useful to the headline writer, is believed to be the first of its kind so compiled.

The importance of the copy editor's function is treated elsewhere. Suffice it to set down here that the authors consider it to be the backbone of the newspaper and, as such, deserving of a book all its own. Editorial writers may, within their limited confines, be brilliant and persuasive; reporters may be enterprising and thorough; but it is the copy editors who have in their keeping ultimately the newspaper's reputation for accuracy, for attractiveness and for intelligence.

The authors acknowledge a debt to colleagues who have given wise counsel on the contents of this book, but who, in the true newspaper tradition, are content to "keep their names out of print." The authors feel, however, that especial thanks are due to the late Professor Charles P. Cooper, of the Columbia School of Journalism, who suggested the book and guided and inspired its preparation.

The cable copy and proofs are reproduced from those of *The New York Times.*

R. E. G.

T. M. B.

New York

CONTENTS

PART ONE. COPY

I. NEWSPAPER ORGANIZATION

THE EMPHASIS in newspaper work has long—too long, perhaps—been put upon the reporter. While there is no wish to take from him credit for his many superb contributions to the excellence of the modern newspaper, it ought to be realized that there is a man who stands between him and his critical public—the copy editor. The sparkling, swift, entertaining story, signed by John Jones of *The Daily Star*, draws comment and approbation, but it is not often recognized, even by his fellows, that the copy editor's share in the creation of the gem may be as great as if not greater than that of John Jones, reporter.

It is not seldom that the wit, ingenuity and craftsmanship of the copy editor rescue from the limbo of unread newspaper stories the uninspired work of John Jones. It is the editorial pencil as much as the reportorial typewriter that puts before the public daily the readable information of the world's happenings. It is the copy editor who is essentially the guardian of what gets into the newspaper and how it looks when it gets there. He detects the errors, corrects the English, cuts out the dead wood of verbiage, tones the story up to its proper pitch or down to the level required by good taste or the libel laws.

The appeal of the reporter's work is great; the activity, the contact with the world, with its great men and with its ideas, make the stimulation of the job unparalleled in any profession. But the copy editor is closer to the heart of the newspaper's power; he is indeed, its heart. Under his pencil flow the accounts of all important happenings anywhere. This sense of closeness to vital things, plus the ability to shape information about them so that their importance will be shown in true perspective, make the copy desk job second to none.

Whatever the respective merits of the copy editor's and the reporter's work, both are cogs in a machine that has only one object: to gather and publish quickly information of events. The newspaper strives to put before its readers daily the interesting and important happenings that have occurred or have become known in the preceding twenty-four hours. Information, to be news, must be new, fresh, immediate, and it is the reporter's task to gather and write it quickly and the copy editor's to hasten it through the news machine into print.

To meet the requirements of his position properly, the copy editor must have a detailed knowledge of the highly developed organization that has been set up to speed copy to his desk and through his hands into type. The machine is linked to all parts of the world by radio, cable, telephone, telegraph, ship, plane and train. Internally the newspaper office is equipped to transfer words from copy to print in minutes. The effort is perpetual to draw widespread information to a focal point and send it out again as a newspaper.

Not only is speed requisite in the gathering and the printing of the news; it is paramount also in imparting information to the reader. The newspaper story is constructed so that the most information can be told in the least time. To convey its message effectively, the story must be clear, concise, emphatic. The important facts must come first, the less important follow in their order. The headline, likewise, is a device to tell the news quickly. It is a further condensation of a story that has already been stripped to its essentials in the introduction. The headline must be specific and forceful. Excess must be shorn away; facts must be set forth to the point of baldness.

It must not be supposed that this speed is uncontrolled; it is that of efficient men trained to their work. It is not achieved at the expense of thoroughness or accuracy, without which their efforts would be valueless.

THE MANAGING EDITOR

At the head of the news organization is the managing editor. From him or through him comes the driving force that keeps the machine at its most efficient point. On him depends the morale of the organization.

His chief efforts are concerned with news gathering. He is informed of the world's events and, through his subordinate editors, obtains accounts of these happenings for the newspaper's readers. Essentially his object is simple; actually the attainment of that object is extremely complex. His plans cannot be hit or miss; they must be laid with minute care. It is in this that the qualities of the managing editor are shown to the best advantage.

For example, let it be supposed that the newspaper prints a small story of an outbreak of hostilities in Cuba. This item is read by the managing editor as a routine part of his duties. Has it possibilities? Is it worth while to send a special correspondent to watch the situation? A decision on this will depend very little on the facts given in the story. It will depend rather on his knowledge of the general conditions in Cuba, whether these are such that there might be further disorders, what effect such violence might have on the island itself and what effect it might have on the relations of the United States with Cuba and Cuba's with other nations. Answers to such questions hinge not upon the immediate situation, but upon the managing editor's store of historical knowledge about the country and its problems. It hinges also on his sensing of possibilities, in short on his news sense.

If he decides to send a correspondent, his next problem is to select the right man. The assignment is a delicate and a responsible one, perhaps even dangerous. The choice must be wise. In making it, he relies on his knowledge of his staff's abilities and character. Success or failure in obtaining a story often depends on selecting the right man for the assignment.

His next step is getting the reporter to the scene, equipped with detailed instructions, if necessary, of what to do. This is often vital in order to maintain contact between the office and the reporter. How to send stories is frequently a major difficulty. There may be a censorship, or for other reasons communication may be erratic. Various plans should be considered, leaving it to the reporter to make the best of whatever situation he finds.

Covering a national election is another major problem of organization. A vast temporary framework of communication with all parts of the country must be set up. Correspondents in strategic places must be obtained and instructed in detail concerning what information to send and when to send it. This is a task that requires several months. The outline of the campaign is worked out by the managing editor and his assistants put it into effect.

This is the field work. The managing editor must also prepare his office organization for election day or election night. New, temporary schedules for editors, reporters, copy editors, composing room and pressroom forces must be thought out in detail. Virtually the whole machine must be shifted about for the handling of one vast news story. When this is completed and the machine begins to function on election day or night, the managing editor takes full charge of the editing, make-up and printing.

The successful managing editor plans to meet difficulties before they arise. He does not rely solely on one plan; he lays alternate plans for use if the most promising fails. If he cannot get the information he wants from one source he gets it from another; if he cannot get it at one time, he does not shelve the idea as impossible, but waits and obtains it when possible.

It is a mistaken idea that an editor is a man who wields a pencil over copy paper. Editing is rather the selection of news, knowing what events are the most vital and most worth covering. This is the managing editor's role. He studies events and brings to the newspaper reader news of those that are interesting and important.

THE CHIEF EDITORS

Downward from the managing editor spreads the organization to reporters and correspondents, the gatherers of news, upon whom the whole newspaper structure rests. His immediate assistants are the city, national and foreign editors; the first directing the gathering of the news in the city where the newspaper is published and in its immediate vicinity; the second, the gathering of the news in the United States outside of the city of publication; and the third, the gathering of the news in foreign countries. Other editors assisting him are the heads of specialized departments such as financial and business, sports and society.

On a large morning newspaper there are duplicate editors for day and night to cover the span of the paper's operation, the day editors generally carrying the chief title and the burden of the position. This is by no means the common system, but it illustrates the thorough covering and editing of news by departments, and the functions, if not the individual editors, exist in most city newspaper organizations. For example, most newspapers do not maintain foreign news-gathering facilities, but the function of the foreign editor remains, whether on the day or the night staff. A newspaper that does not have a foreign staff may have a single correspondent in any center abroad, or it may rely on the wire services.

Likewise in the succeeding pages the copy-desk system is divided into three—city, national and foreign—for illustrative purposes, whereas the general practice is either to combine the national and foreign copy desks or to set up a "universal" desk on which all copy is edited.

The City Editor. In the home city of the newspaper and in its vicinity the news-gathering machinery is elaborate. Since the business life of the newspaper is sustained by the community in which it exists, and since the greater part of its circulation is there, local news must be covered in great detail. For the same reason, a substantial part of the news that is printed is of local origin.

At the head of this part of the machine is the city editor. News judgment, executive ability and a store of information of names and events are his chief qualifications. He should know his city, not only its geography, but also its history; the masses of its people as well as its important residents. He need not have encyclopedic knowledge, but the background against which he views the world should be broad and human. This is apart from his ability to know news when he hears of it. News judgment is not essentially a thinking process; it is an instinct built upon many things forgotten.

If a local disaster occurs, it is the city editor's task to get his reporters to the scene quickly. Not only must they be at the spot, but each also must have a clear idea of the precise part he is to play in gathering the details of the event. It is the city editor's function to instruct each man fully and clearly, so that no confusion will result and so that every angle of the story will be covered. Not all the reporters will write what they see or the facts they gather. The editor must pick his best men for that purpose; the others will get information, investigate and report their findings to the men who will organize and write the stories.

For example, a train wreck would be divided into the following angles: the story of the accident itself; stories of eyewitnesses or passengers; the engineer's story; the list of injured, or of the dead and the injured; the color story of the scene; photographs of the scene. In addition, if any were killed, or if any of the injured or dead were important persons, queries would be sent to various places for information regarding them. Here, then, are eight angles, each of which will require at least one reporter and some of them several. Other angles might crop up as information regarding the accident reaches the city editor. If the wreck is a serious one, another reporter would be assigned to write a story of past similar accidents.

The reporter who is to write the leading story of the accident should be sent to the scene if time permits; if time is short, he should remain in the newspaper office and take information by telephone from the reporters on the ground. It is his duty to organize the mass of detail that comes to him. The subsidiary stories are written by the reporters sent to the scene, if they have time to gather the facts and return to the office; otherwise they also telephone the facts to rewrite men.

It is a sudden development, like the foregoing illustration, that tests the city editor. It creates a problem that must first be visualized; then a course of action must be mapped out, and then action taken swiftly and with certainty. His plan of campaign depends on the size and abilities of his staff. If he has few reporters, each must be assigned carefully to obtain the best results; if he has many, the task is more easily and more thoroughly accomplished. But if his plan is loose and ill-conceived and the disposition of his men inefficient, the result will be confusion.

The assignment sheet is the city editor's chart. On it is designated each story that is to be covered and the name of the reporter assigned to cover it. Every reporter is informed daily, usually orally, but also by note, what his assignment is to be. This chart serves also as the city editor's record of the disposition of all men under his supervision.

Much news is of spontaneous origin. In such cases the city editor is dependent on his reporters in strategic posts to learn of the event and inform him. He relies also upon the news services and upon outside sources. Any event anywhere is reported eventually in the newspaper office, as well as rumors of much that never has happened. In general, however, the newspaper safeguards itself by posting men in places where news ordinarily originates. Future scheduled events are recorded in a "futures" file, on which the city editor relies in the routine of planning assignments. These records may be newspaper clippings, announcements issued by the organizations concerned or publicity agents' copy.

The staff of reporters of a large newspaper may range from a score to a hundred. Many of them are specialists, versed in particular fields, such as public utilities, politics, labor questions, religious matters, aviation or art; others are feature writers, skilled in describing events colorfully, imparting the flavor as well as reporting the facts; still others are general assignment men, able to cover any occurrence efficiently and completely.

There are reporters with fixed assignments or beats, such as those covering the courts, city hall and other public buildings. It is these men who produce most of the day's news, for they are placed in the spots where news ordinarily originates. Other reporters are assigned regularly to police headquarters and to various districts throughout the city, whose duty it is to report spontaneous stories, to be alert for any news development, and to verify or to cover any angle of stories developing elsewhere.

Surburban correspondents constitute a considerable part of the city editor's staff. They are reporters in outlying towns or cities, often employed directly by the metropolitan newspaper, but usually employed by newspapers in their own communities. The city editor keeps in touch with them by telephone, generally ordering stories but sometimes accepting also those that the correspondent has covered on his own initative.

National and Foreign Editors. As the source of news recedes from the home office, the scantier become the means of reporting. Thus the day national and foreign staffs are similar to but far less complex than the day city staff organization. The national and foreign editors act in a supervisory or directing capacity only. Removed from the scenes of action, they can advise merely or give orders by means of telephone, telegraph or cable.

The larger newspapers have established bureaus or maintain correspondents in many cities of the United States, notably in Washington. The Washington correspondent of a large newspaper is a directing news gatherer, virtually a city editor with a staff of reporters under his control. He is to a large extent independent of the home office and is responsible for covering the news fully in his city.

Spread over the country, however, in all important centers and in many minor cities, are scores of correspondents who supply stories of news events in their territories only on request, or only after asking the home office whether the story is desired and how much to send. Scanning the domestic field and ordering stories is, in general, the function of the national editor.

In the same manner the foreign editor controls the gathering of news abroad. Still farther from the scene of action, his duties are even more generalized than those of the national editor. As in the case of the Washington correspondent, the heads of bureaus in capitals abroad act as city editors in the cities where they are stationed and as national editors for the countries. Under each is a staff, generally small, of reporters familiar with the country concerned and with its politics and language. The foreign editor in the home office exercises general oversight over the whole foreign field. Not the least of his duties is keeping watch on the skeletonizing by correspondents abroad of cable copy, which, when properly done, may save the newspaper many thousands of dollars yearly in cable tolls.

THE "NIGHT SIDE"

These chief editors gather or direct the gathering of most of the news. In the late afternoon the "night side," whose functions are to edit and to print the newspaper, takes control.

Each editor is duplicated at night by an editor whose duties are similar, although modern practice is to fix hours of duty so that the responsible executive is available during the vital hours of news gathering and editing. Thus there is an over-all night executive, usually called the news editor, with a number of assistants, varying with the size of the newspaper, who exercises general control over the gathering of news of events happening at night and over the editing, placing and printing of all news stories.

The process of "taking over" by the night staff is important, since it is vital that no break occur between the day and the night activities. In the case of the city editor, this is accomplished by the transferring of the assignment sheet by the day editor to his night counterpart, the record itself being supplemented by oral explanations of the covering or the treatment of stories. In the case of the national and foreign editors, no personal transfer takes place, except in special situations, but the night men, by scanning the messages that have been sent and received, obtain a picture of what has been done during the day.

The Night Editors. Assuming all the responsibilities of the city editor, his night assistant in addition has control of the writing of most of the news, including that covered during the day, a function little exercised by the day executive. He tells the reporter how much space he may have and, if necessary, how to construct the story.

His staff is supplemented also by reporters covering specified districts, duplicating the day system, and by rewrite men who take the facts of stories over the telephone from district men or correspondents and who write the stories. The latter usually take advantage of shorthand or symbols developed by themselves to facilitate the process of getting news by telephone. Generally they have been graduated from the ranks of reporters and frequently have unusual gifts of imagination. To draw out a story from the reporter at the scene, to organize it in the mind quickly, to grasp at once its news features and value, require experience and ingenuity of a high order.

Under the night editor's direction also is the city copy desk, made up of a head of the desk and copy editors. With the night editor begins the process of editing the news, which is continued to completion by the copy editors.

A similar system is in effect for both the national and foreign staffs. For these night editors the foreign and domestic bureaus and correspondents make up the reporting staffs. The aid of reporters on the night city staff, however, is frequently asked by these editors to rewrite a story that is not properly written by their correspondents and to provide background material from clippings or other sources for out-of-town stories.

Afternoon newspapers have the same general organization, as to function at any rate. But their problems differ and are multiplied because they are reporting, editing and publishing during the day hours when news events are occurring. Assignments of their reporting staff are similar to those of morning newspaper procedure but the bulk of their news content is produced by rewrite men from facts telephoned by reporters at the scene. They must keep up, edition by edition, with developments as they occur. They work by telephone largely, shift their display of stories as their staff reports, play the "spot news" hard. They lack time for a moderate period of reflection and judgment of the relative value of news occurrences. Their executive staff also is less elaborate than that of the large morning paper, the functions being concentrated in fewer men.

The remaining important night executive is the make-up editor. As the liaison man between the news room and the composing room, he has authority in both departments and is subordinate only to the night editor in charge and his assistants. His chief concerns are to place stories properly in reference to the space required by advertisements and to typographical appearance, and to get the paper to press on time. Working from dummy pages that indicate the placing and the space occupied by display advertisements and from galley proofs of news stories, he organizes the page layouts and indicates to the composing-room force where the news stories are to ap-

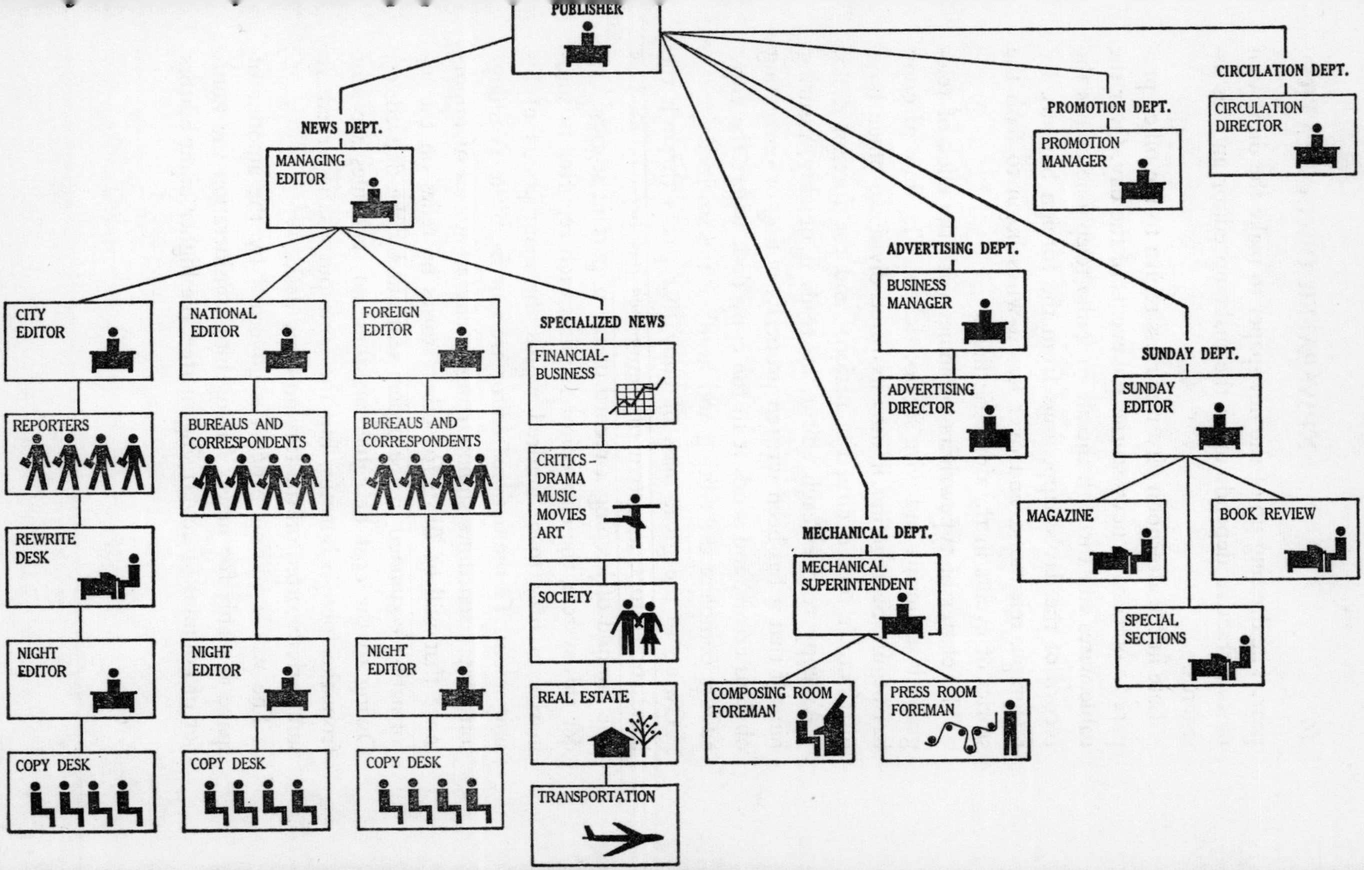
PUBLISHER
NEWS DEPT.
MANAGING EDITOR
CITY EDITOR
REPORTERS
REWRITE DESK
NIGHT EDITOR
COPY DESK
NATIONAL EDITOR
BUREAUS AND CORRESPONDENTS
NIGHT EDITOR
COPY DESK
FOREIGN EDITOR
BUREAUS AND CORRESPONDENTS
NIGHT EDITOR
COPY DESK
SPECIALIZED NEWS
FINANCIAL-BUSINESS
CRITICS - DRAMA MUSIC MOVIES ART
SOCIETY
REAL ESTATE
TRANSPORTATION
MECHANICAL DEPT.
MECHANICAL SUPERINTENDENT
COMPOSING ROOM FOREMAN
PRESS ROOM FOREMAN
ADVERTISING DEPT.
BUSINESS MANAGER
ADVERTISING DIRECTOR
SUNDAY DEPT.
SUNDAY EDITOR
MAGAZINE
BOOK REVIEW
SPECIAL SECTIONS
PROMOTION DEPT.
PROMOTION MANAGER
CIRCULATION DEPT.
CIRCULATION DIRECTOR

pear. The dressing up of the newspaper to make the display of news attractive depends upon the make-up editor and his assistants.

Late in the afternoon city reporters return to the office prepared to record in news stories the events of the day. Over the cable wires and through the air by radio telephone comes the record of the day's happenings from the foreign bureaus. By telegraph, telephone, and over leased wires begin to flash the stories of events in the domestic field.

The clatter of typewriters combines with the click of telegraph instruments and wire service tickers. The flow of copy has begun. Segregating it into its three divisions, office boys distribute it to the city, the national and the foreign desks.

As copy reaches each editor, he reads it quickly, assuring himself that it has been written properly, noting or correcting obvious errors, and sends it to the copy desk where the copy editors complete the editing and headline the stories.

Owing to the great mass of copy that passes through the hands of editors, a system of summaries has been devised as one method of keeping a record of the important stories. Under this system, the city editor requires each reporter to summarize in fifty to a hundred words the main points of his assignment. To the national editor are sent from the Washington bureau schedules summarizing briefly all stories of importance that will be filed; for other stories he relies on the information contained in the orders sent out by the day editor. Owing to the cost of cable messages, no schedules are sent from the foreign bureaus, but the same purpose is served by summaries written on the foreign copy desk.

The whole editing process is governed by the amount of space available for news. Taking into consideration the number of columns of advertising matter, the higher night editors determine the total allotment for news. The number of pages for an issue is fixed in consultation with the advertising department and is normally based on past experience for the day or season. The average news content tends to become standardized. The ratio of advertising to news is variable and it is neither a good business nor a good editorial policy to establish a fixed ratio. The tendency is to expand the newspaper when the volume of news and of advertising is large and to contract it when the volume of both is small. If, however, the volume of advertising is small, the news space is not necessarily reduced in order to keep down the size of the paper. The size is fixed by daily conditions. In most offices the minimum routine requirement for news space stays at about the same level and is rarely cut drastically; on the other hand it frequently is expanded if the news volume makes that course necessary.

The space allotted for news is divided among city, national and foreign editors, each receiving approximately the amount that he estimates he will require. Each editor is guided by this allotment in judging the space that may be given to any story.

SUPPLEMENTARY DEPARTMENTS

In the estimate of total news columns, allowance must be made also for other departments, operating semi-independently of the news department, but under the supervision of the night editors. Among these are the society department, which has a separate staff of reporters to gather its news and sometimes a separate desk to edit it; the sports department, also made up of reporters versed in sports matters and specialized copy editors; the financial and business department, composed of writers and copy editors who are authorities in their field; the theater department, made up of drama and motion picture critics; the music department, comprising the critics of music

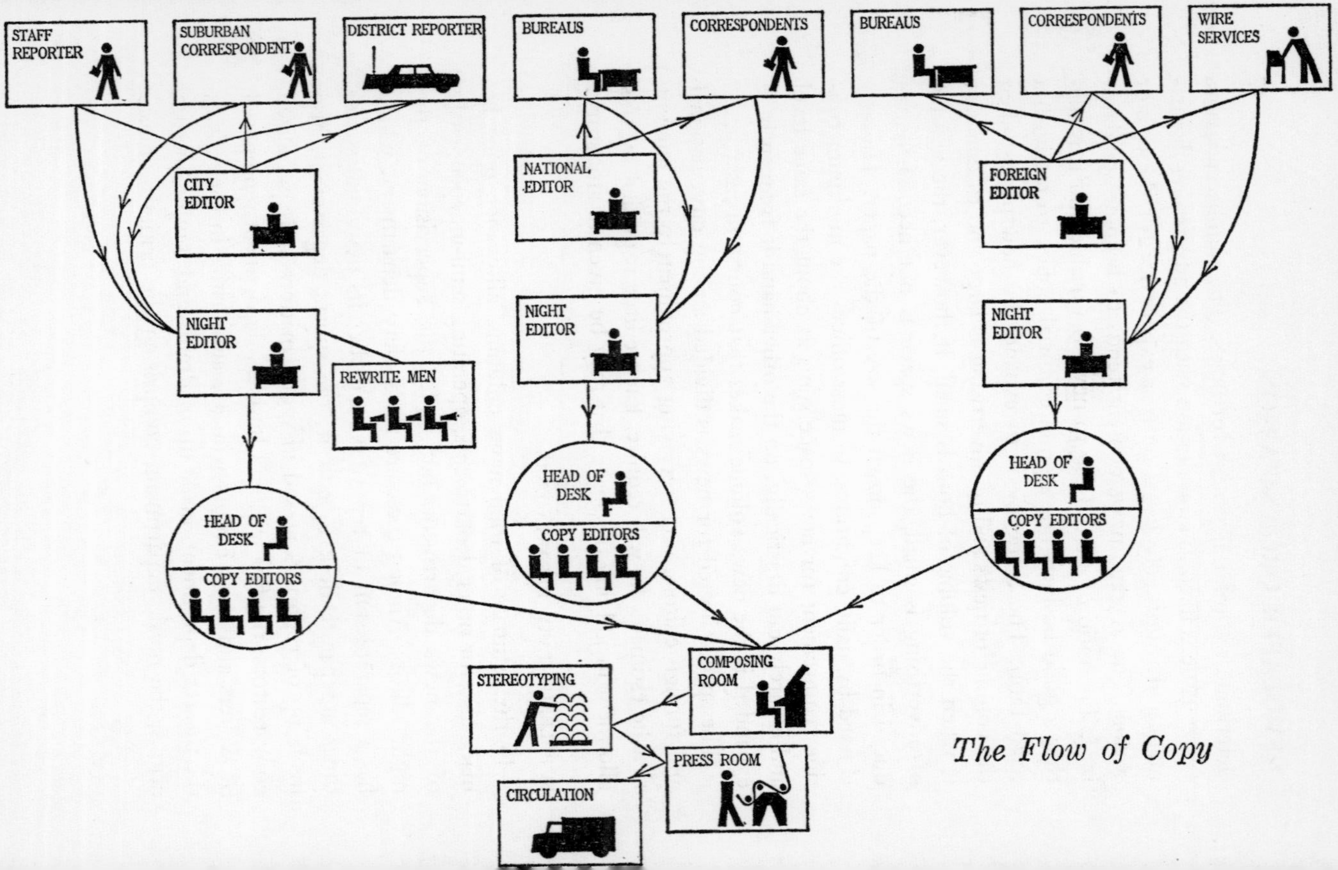

The Flow of Copy

and reporters of news in this field; the art news department, which may include an art critic as well as a reporter of news in the art world; and the book news department, covering news of the publishing field as well as book criticism.

These divisions range from one-man departments on smaller newspapers to departments employing a score or more persons, each with a specialized task, on the large newspapers. The division of the newspaper organization depends entirely upon its size and resources. The news of each department may be edited by semi-independent copy desks made up of special copy editors, but usually all copy goes to the general copy desks and is edited in the same manner as general news copy. The product of all these departments is news and differs not at all from general news in importance. News is departmentalized solely to facilitate the gathering and to insure expert treatment. Allotment of space for departmental news is made at the same time as that for general news.

Space must be allotted also for pictures, the amount depending on the newspaper's policy. If news pictures or photographs of persons are desired, a news picture service, perhaps maintained by the newspaper itself, supplies them, and the cuts are made either by the newspaper's own art department or by outside plants specializing in such work.

THE FRONT PAGE

From the great number of stories that enter the newspaper office in a single night, ten to fifteen or more must be selected for the front page. In some offices this responsibility falls upon one of the assistants to the night editor in charge, and it is to facilitate his work that the summaries of news stories are kept. In other offices the conference system is used, under which the city, national and foreign editors confer with the higher executives, and recommend for the first page their chief stories. In this case, summaries are unnecessary.

Many stories are obviously first-page stories; others are doubtful. On the latter, conferences may be held by the editor in charge of the task with his colleagues or superior. If there are more stories of sufficient importance to be displayed on the front page than space permits, they must be weighed against one another. The ten or fifteen or more stories must be weighed to determine their relative importance so that they may be displayed in that order.

The columns of the first page generally are rated, as to display value in a regular one-column head make-up, in the following order: 8, 1 or 6, 3, 7, 5, 4, 2. The right-hand side above the fold of the paper is the best display space because that quarter of the newspaper can be seen if the paper is folded on the newsstand. Because of this, column 6 has excellent display value, although column 1 is generally considered to be the best after column 8. Nowadays newspapers are placed flat on the newsstand but this does not alter the values materially. Columns 1, 3, 6 and 8 are considered to have more display value than columns 2, 4, 5 and 7 because the former require "top heads," that is, headlines that extend up to the top of the page and are therefore larger, while the stories in the latter columns usually appear with smaller headlines under boxes or pictures. The editor who selects first-page stories must consider balance also, and so place one-column and two-column boxes, cuts, maps and other typographical devices so that the display is attractive. This is especially important when the leading story in column 8 requires a headline that spreads over two, three or more columns. Such a layout frequently alters the display value of the columns and requires special care in balancing the whole page. Balance does not necessarily mean regularity, which may serve only to diminish the display value of the whole page. In addition to the chief stories selected for the first page, minor short stories may also be used to break up long columns of type or to give a pleasing effect of irregularity.

The front page of a morning newspaper may not change from first edition to last, but the afternoon newspaper, with perhaps six editions, is likely to change the first page make-up for each edition. This is because the afternoon paper is being published while most of the day's news events are occurring and continual shifting of stories is necessary to keep pace with events. The early or "bulldog" edition of an afternoon newspaper may contain chiefly the same stories that appeared in the late editions of the morning newspapers in a rewritten form and as new events occur the early stories are shifted from the first page to the inside of the paper and from the forward pages to the back until finally the least important drop out and the more important are retained on less conspicuous pages, unless new developments enhance their value.

THE COMPOSING ROOM

While the writing and editing of copy go forward continuously and quickly in the news room, the composing room, where the news is set in type and the newspaper is made up, goes slowly into operation. Here great batteries of linotype machines clatter, spewing down bright lines of type. With amazing speed, galley after galley is filled with type as stories are set and assembled. Each galley of type is inked, a number of proofs taken and the type is placed on a bank where it lies, except for corrections, until time for the paper to be made up.

The composing room sets first the type that appears in the back pages of the newspaper, such as the agate tables of financial news, the stock-exchange quotations and the shipping news. It works forward to the general news.

After the type is set by the compositors, copy and a galley proof go to the proof room, an adjunct of the mechanical department. Here the proof is checked against the copy and all typographical errors that appear in the proof are corrected by notations in the margin. The proofreader's duty is to "follow copy" and to correct typographical errors, although he may refer questions of fact back to the news room. After this checking up process, the corrected proof is returned to the composing room and every line in which a mistake occurs is reset. Printers insert the corrected lines in their proper position, removing at the same time the incorrect lines.

THE DEADLINE APPROACHES

By the time the first page make-up has been determined, the deadline for the first edition is approaching. Dummies of the front page go to the city, national and foreign editors and to the make-up editor. Guided by it, the copy desks write the proper headlines for the designated stories. Proofs from the composing room have been distributed, read, corrected if necessary and the stories reduced in length if required. The make-up editor and his assistants, informed as to the news and the length of stories by means of proofs, go to the composing room.

Here in rows are long benches, known as "stones," with level tops of metal. On each are iron rectangular frames, called chases, in which the type is placed. When a chase is filled with type, constituting a page, the whole is called a form. Under the direction of the make-up editors, printers place in these frames the type that has been accumulating on the type banks. Long stories are placed first; the vacant spaces are then filled with short stories, or, if the vacant space is small, the type is leaded. In the making up of each page, balance always should be considered when the advertising layout permits, and long stretches of type should be broken up by the judicious placing of boxes, cuts of various kinds and by headlines of contrasting type. As soon as a page form is completed, it is closed and the type clamped, by means of screws in the edge of the frame, so that the type cannot shift or fall out.

The make-up work proceeds in relays by fixed schedule. Some newspapers set an early deadline for the financial news so that the back pages are out of the way when the rush of general news make-up begins. The schedule may call for the closing of from four to sixteen page forms every twenty minutes, depending on the number of pages in the issue and on the newspaper's size and facilities. Each page form, when closed, is removed from the stone to a pressure machine for the making of a matrix, which is an impression of the type on a heavy papier-mâché sheet. This matrix, or "mat," is conveyed to the stereotyping room where a metal cast is made. The cast, which prints that page of the newspaper, is then clamped to the rotary press.

The first page form usually is the last to be filled. At times pages are held for a few minutes in order to get into the first edition a last-minute story, but delay is avoided when possible. The time of the deadline has been set to meet circulation requirements and a few minutes lost in the composing room may cause tardy deliveries at trains for distribution in the suburbs and elsewhere.

When the first page is closed, the printer's mallet, pounding the type surface to make sure that no stray line of type projects above the general level, gives the signal that the edition has been "put to bed."

As in the case of preceding pages, a mat and a cast are made of the first page and the cast is put on the press. If the newspaper is large, duplicate casts are made so that several of the great rotary presses can print the newspaper at the same time, each at the rate of some 50,000 an hour.

The First Edition. After the first edition deadline has been passed, a temporary lull settles on the news room. Then the vibration of the great presses can be felt. In a few minutes the first edition, still wet and smelling of printer's ink, comes up from the pressroom. It is corrected, cut and added to. The second edition is the next goal. It appears soon afterward, and the first is already history.

If the organization of a large newspaper seems to be so complex as to be bewildering, it can be pointed out that this complexity is more apparent than real. The functions are simple. The editor of a small paper in a county seat does the same work on a smaller scale. If he solicits his own advertising, he is functioning as the business department. He is his own reporter, collecting and writing local news; he is the copy editor and headline writer; he is the managing editor and make-up editor; the editorial writer and probably the compositor and printer and pressman and distributor. If he has correspondents throughout the county and a state or national wire service he is a national editor; and if his paper is large enough to have a fuller world service, he becomes a foreign editor also.

If his paper should grow, requiring the adding of employees, he would begin the division of labor and the functions of gathering, editing and printing news would be distributed among several persons. He would meet new conditions with a more complex organization, just as the large newspaper expands its structure to meet the conditions of keen competition and demands for speed.

2. THE COPY EDITOR

ERRORS creep into newspaper copy from many sources. News passes through many hands; it is garbled in transmission; it is written and rewritten by men of varied ages, education and temperament; it is read and edited under similar conditions. Wrong perspective or partisanship, too much enthusiasm or too little, may handicap a story. The very speed with which newspapers must be printed permits mistakes to slip by the many persons who handle news in its course through the news machine. The continuous struggle of the newspaper is to eliminate errors. Many checks have been set up against them and the chief of these is the copy editor.

THE IMPORTANCE OF THE COPY EDITOR

The copy editor is virtually the last man between his newspaper and the public. The copy may have been read several times before it reaches him, but its ultimate form, phraseology and spirit rest in his hands. Mistakes or poor writing that pass him are almost certain to reach the reader in print. They may be detected in the office in time to be corrected, but many such blunders are never discovered except by the newspaper reader.

The greatest weapon of the copy editor in his efforts to eliminate errors is an alertness that challenges every fact, every name, virtually every word. Every fact should be checked. Those that appear incorrect and cannot be verified must be eliminated. Statements that are absurd or dangerous are deleted without question. Likewise the facts should be weighed against one another to assure consistency.

The function of the copy editor is critical, not creative. In no circumstances should he rewrite a story completely. If it cannot be saved except by being rewritten, that work should be done by a rewrite man or by the reporter who wrote the original story. The desk man must cope with the material that is given him and make the most of it by recasting, striking out superfluous words, substituting active or colorful words for dead ones, expressing a phrase in a word and by other similar means.

The finished product should be concise, forceful, complete. This should be the copy editor's aim with every story, not merely with the important ones. A great news story virtually tells itself; it is the brief stories that most often are allowed to slip by with only a few strokes of the pencil to indicate that they have been read. Any story can be improved, even though the editing consists of transposing a word, shifting a punctuation mark, substituting a concrete word for a general one, or an Anglo-Saxon verb for a Latin one.

Leaving unaltered one word that should be changed is not a trivial matter. The careful copy editor leaves nothing to chance. His object is not only to correct errors, but also to improve.

With a unanimity that is somewhat disconcerting to the copy editor, reporters profess to regard him as a mutilator of good copy and there is some ground for this opinion. There are some desk men temperamentally unfitted to make the most of another man's writing; their conception of what a story should be is so strong that virtual rewriting is the only course they can follow. Such men must be restrained, and, if they remain copy editors, trained to the viewpoint of the editorial pencil rather than to that of the reportorial typewriter. The general aim of the copy desk is to preserve as far as possible the words of the reporter, if they express what he desires to convey, and to retain the spirit imparted by him, if it is proper. As the final link in a long and expensive process, the copy editor can destroy the honest work of many reporters.

The business of writing and editing news is a cooperative undertaking, demanding the best of many brains. There is no place for pride of authorship. The desk man should recognize and retain the merits of the story given to him to edit, the reporter should realize that the copy editor often saves him from grave mistakes and generally improves his work.

The Copy Desk. The copy desk usually is semicircular or horseshoe-shaped. The head of the desk sits at the center of the inside curve and his position is known as the "slot," and he himself, sometimes, as the "slot man." The copy editors sit "on the rim."

Copy comes to the head of the desk, who reads it to form an opinion of the required headline information, edits it as closely as he wishes, and passes it to one of the copy editors. When the copy has been edited in detail and headlined, it is returned to the head of the desk. If the edited copy and the headline meet with his approval, both are sent to the composing room. If there is criticism of either, the necessary corrections are made in the copy or the headline is rewritten or rephrased.

In giving copy to his editors the head of the desk takes into consideration their abilities or their special knowledge. Like reporters, there are some who are experts in special fields, such as politics, labor questions, railroads, art or literature; others are especially adept at writing feature headlines and still others are able to cope with stories of any kind. Some are slow, careful editors; others are quick as well as accurate. Speed is a necessity when the deadline draws near.

How the copy editor deals with copy and headlines is described at length in subsequent chapters. His approach to the task depends largely on his abilities. A good method in the case of a long or a complicated story is to read the copy once simply for information and to gain a general idea of its structure. Probably in this reading any obvious inconsistencies in facts or faults in construction will be detected and corrected, by editing in the former case and by rearrangement in the latter. The next step is a second reading for close editing, with attention to the standards set forth later. A third reading of the edited copy, while not necessary in many instances, is an additional safeguard to assure a product as finished as it lies in the power of the copy editor to achieve.

Cable copy offers another problem, different from that of editing local or telegraph copy. This is owing to the practice of skeletonizing stories before they are cabled in order to reduce the expense. Often cable copy is so cryptic because of faulty skeletonizing as to become a baffling puzzle. In such cases, the background of the editor, his knowledge of the situation dealt with, is invaluable.

Not until the copy has been carefully corrected, is the copy editor in a position to consider the headline. His alterations may modify the point of view or qualify the statement of the facts in such a way that a headline built on the original copy would have been incorrect or distorted. When the editing is completed it is often helpful as preparation for writing the headline for the editor mentally to stand away from the story so that he may view it as a whole rather than in detail. This method is not necessarily to determine the news point, which at this stage should be obvious, but to discover the most effective way to tell the news in the headline; whether, for example, to write a broad, all-inclusive headline or a narrow, more specific one that singles out one phase of the story.

The Copy Editor's Background. The education, experience and knowledge of the copy editor cannot be too broad. The more he has learned, seen or knows, the greater his value to the newspaper. He should have a wide knowledge of names, places and events; he must be well-informed in the arts, sciences and social trends; he should know history and literature and be familiar with the machinery of governments and law.

It is imperative that he be acquainted with his own city, if he is an editor of local copy. He must know its geography, its people, its government, its officials, its buildings. If he is an editor of national copy, he must have a wide knowledge of national politics, movements, figures and events. Copy editors dealing with legislation in the national or in state capitals should have detailed information about the machinery of legislatures. If the editor is dealing with foreign copy he must know much about the politics, economics and government of the countries concerned and of their recent history at least. Finally the copy editor must have common sense. The logic he uses to test the reasonableness of assertions in news stories is the same logic he applies in everyday affairs.

THE VALUE OF REFERENCE BOOKS

Whatever the store of information, memory cannot always be trusted. It is necessary to verify. Familiarity with the common reference books is invaluable to the copy editor. If he does not know or cannot recall a name, a date, or any other fact, he should know where they can be found. It is worthwhile for every copy editor to investigate the reference shelves of his office so that he can put his hand on the proper book quickly. Most newspapers have "morgues" where newspaper and sometimes other clippings concerning events and persons are filed. Many questions of fact can be determined quickly by reference to these clippings. Some newspapers also have libraries where difficulties on questions more remote than those ordinarily arising in editorial work can be settled.

Some of the more common reference books are the following:

DICTIONARIES (Not only for definitions and spelling, but also for historical names and dates. Foreign dictionaries often are helpful.)

ENCYCLOPEDIAS

TELEPHONE DIRECTORIES (for spelling of names and for home locations)

CITY DIRECTORIES (for spelling of names, home locations and businesses)

THE COLUMBIA-LIPPINCOTT GAZETTEER (for place names, locations and geographical descriptions)

THE WORLD ALMANAC (for general factual information)

NEW YORK TIMES INDEX

WHO'S WHO IN AMERICA

WHO'S WHO

WHO'S WHO IN NEW YORK

WHO'S WHO IN MUSIC

WHO'S WHO IN ART

WHO'S WHO IN LITERATURE

WHO'S WHO IN CANADA

WHO'S WHO IN AUSTRALIA

WHO'S WHO IN THE NATION'S CAPITAL

WHO'S WHO IN GOVERNMENT (statesmen of the world)

WHO'S WHO IN JURISPRUDENCE (United States and elsewhere)

WHO'S WHO IN MUSIC AND DRAMA

WHO'S WHO IN BRITISH AVIATION

WHO'S WHO IN FINANCE, BANKING AND INSURANCE

WER IST'S (Who's Who of Germany)

EUROPA (European Year Book)

QUI ÊTES-VOUS? (Who's Who of France)

STATESMEN'S YEAR BOOK
MUSIC YEAR BOOK
YEAR BOOK OF AGRICULTURE
AMERICAN LABOR YEAR BOOK
AMERICAN YEAR BOOK (record of events and progress)
AMERICAN MEN OF SCIENCE (biographical dictionary)
LEGISLATIVE MANUAL (New York State)
BURKE'S PEERAGE, BARONETAGE AND KNIGHTAGE (names and ranks of the Royal Family and the British nobility)
DEBRETT'S PEERAGE, BARONETAGE, KNIGHTAGE AND COMPANIONAGE
SOCIAL REGISTER (names and family connections of prominent persons)
POOR'S INDUSTRIAL COMPANIES (list of corporations, officers and financial data)
POOR'S PUBLIC UTILITIES
POOR'S RAILROADS
POOR'S REGISTER OF DIRECTORS
MOODY'S INDUSTRIALS
MOODY'S RAILROADS
MOODY'S PUBLIC UTILITIES
DIRECTORY OF DIRECTORS (officers of corporations in New York)
JANE'S FIGHTING SHIPS (general and technical information about warships throughout the world)
JANE'S ALL THE WORLD'S AIRCRAFT
ARMY REGISTER (list of officers, active and retired)
NAVY REGISTER
LLOYD'S REGISTER OF SHIPPING (names and facts about commercial ships)
RECORD OF AMERICAN AND FOREIGN SHIPPING

The habit of reading newspapers, particularly his own, is necessary to the copy editor as well as to editors and reporters. To know what the new development of a continuing story is, it is necessary to know what has been printed. It seems elementary that the newspaper man should know what is in his own newspaper, but many are careless in this respect. The copy editor who does not read it thoroughly is not competent to handle a news story acceptably.

This is especially true for students of journalism. Intelligent reading of the newspapers is the groundwork for any progress they may hope to make in the profession. It is impossible to learn anything about newspapers unless they are read for information and analyzed for technical knowledge.

It is taken for granted that the copy editor knows English grammar and how to write good English. Something more should be required. He should be a student of language because he is to a great extent its guardian. Colloquialisms and slang that are ordinary in speech should be permitted to appear infrequently in newspaper writing. The ultimate value of the copy editor rests solely on his conception of what purpose his newspaper must serve and his ability to help it achieve that end.

3. EDITING THE COPY

THE MISTAKES common to all copy are those of word usage, spelling, punctuation and grammar.

The English used in the newspaper should be that common to all well-educated persons. Language divides naturally into four groups: literary, common, colloquial and slang. Common usage is preferred, because it sets a single standard; the literary is too stilted, although the tendency probably should be toward the literary rather than the colloquial. Slang generally is to be barred.

Discrimination in the use of words is an art. The synonym is convenient but dangerous, and it should be employed with great care. If the copy editor substitutes "assert" for "say," a common practice to obtain variety, he has altered the meaning perceptibly. There is a word to express every action, thought or emotion and it can be found with little difficulty. Synonyms must be used more freely in writing headlines, because of a "rule" against repeating words, but in copy no such freedom should be permitted. Variety can be achieved in many other ways than by abusing the synonym.

Attempts at "fine" or literary writing often lead the reporter into triteness. A few such hackneyed phrases are:

abreast of the times	order out of chaos
was the recipient of	breathless silence
sigh of relief	effect an entrance
in social circles	goes without saying
dull sickening thud	lingering illness

located his whereabouts
news leaked out
much in evidence
beat a hasty retreat
in the business world
was an impressive sight
sadder but wiser
deafening crash
general public
inclemency of the weather
limped into port
lodged in jail
made good his escape
summoned medical aid
blunt instrument
take into custody
crowded to capacity

There are scores of others. The copy editor should change them.

It is absurd also to strain to avoid repetition of words, particularly names; as "capital city" for Washington; "Bay State" for Massachusetts; "the Western metropolis" for any large city in the West.

Directness and simplicity are the easiest ways to avoid such expressions.

PUNCTUATION

Punctuation promotes clarity when properly used. Sentences that need little punctuation, however, are in general the better. To indicate the need of commas and how their use can alter meaning, the following sentences may be studied:

The boys and girls who were on the ground floor escaped.
The boys and girls, who were on the ground floor, escaped.

The man who is an atheist will be imprisoned.
The man, who is an atheist, will be imprisoned.

Fifty delegates who live in New York will be sent.
Fifty delegates, who live in New York, will be sent.

The woman who is a singer is happy.
The woman, who is a singer, is happy.

The mistakes of punctuation most frequent in newspaper copy occur in the use of quotation marks. Every quotation must be closed and the copy editor, on seeing an opening quotation mark, must be certain that the quoted matter is ended with a quotation mark. Quoted passages such as the following appear often in newspapers:

> He said that the purpose of the committee was "to assist in convincing the disaffected that the President is not responsible for the spots on the sun, the storms at sea, the droughts on land, nor the numerous epidemics that frequently sweep sections of the country. Our business is to place him in the minds of the public where his stupendous efforts and brilliant leadership justify. This state reached, there will be no doubt about the results of the contest."

Although this practice is defensible, the better method is to edit the passage as follows:

> He said that the purpose of the committee was "to assist in convincing the disaffected that the President is not responsible for the spots on the sun, the storms at sea, the droughts on land, nor the numerous epidemics that frequently sweep sections of the country."
>
> "Our business is to place him in the minds of the public where his stupendous efforts and brilliant leadership justify," he continued. "This state reached, there will be no doubt about the results of the contest."

It is well to end quoted matter introduced by "he said that" with the phrase, clause or sentence so introduced. Not only does it make the writing clear and more effective, but it also follows the general newspaper rule to set off quoted matter by paragraphs so that it draws attention.

GRAMMAR

Grammatical mistakes are of such great variety that the copy editor or the student of journalism must be referred to the grammars, if he does not have a working knowledge of the rules. The more common blunders, for which the copy editor must be on the alert, are these:

Disagreement in Number Between Subject and Verb. Frequently the verb occurs so far away from the subject that the singular form is used when the subject is plural, or the plural form when the subject is singular. Again confusion may arise when the subject is a clause or when the subject is, for example, "one of the members," or like phrases. The incorrect verbs should be noted in the following illustrations:

The cross-examination of the witness by the defense and the ruling by the court on the admissibility of his evidence *was* put off until tomorrow.

In outlining a set of recommendations for the industry to solve its problems, he warned those who still believe the industry will survive, even if not one of his recommendations *are* carried out, that there is no escaping the truth. . . .

Dangling Participles. In the following illustrations, the first sentence is incorrect, the second and third correct:

Having summed up for two hours, a recess was ordered and the lawyer left.

Having summed up for two hours, the lawyer left after a recess had been ordered.

After he had summed up for two hours, a recess was ordered and the lawyer left.

In the following the dangling participle is at the end:

The two prisoners made a complaint at the station house where they were taken by the policeman alleging extortion.

It should read:

The two prisoners made a complaint, alleging extortion, at the station house where they were taken by the policeman.

Sequence of Tenses. The copy editor should keep close watch on the governing verb (that of the main news story) and relate the tenses of other verbs to it, as determined by the obvious or implied time sequence. The time of the main news story is almost always placed in the past tense. The historical present has become obsolete in newspaper writing.

When the governing verb is in the past, the verbs in clauses dependent upon it also take the past tense, even though the idea of past time does not need to be introduced into the clause. This fact should be kept in mind, for no rule is more commonly violated in newspaper writing. This sequence is called normal sequence, and while the present, or vivid sequence, is often retained in speech, it is not good newspaper practice. For example: "He said that he is well-to-do," is permissible; but "He said that he was well-to-do" is the normal sequence and preferable in newspaper writing.

In the news story the events related almost always are previous in time to that of the governing verb, which, generally, is in the past tense. Therefore, many of the verbs will be necessarily in the past perfect tense to show previous time. In this example the tenses in the clauses are incorrect:

> He testified that he saw the accused man at the scene but that his suspicions were not aroused.

It is obvious that the events the witness is telling about are previous to the time at which he is telling about them. The sentence should read:

> He testified that he had seen the accused man at the scene but that his suspicions had not been aroused.

Frequently this construction is met with in newspaper writing:

> He saw the accused man at the scene, he testified, but his suspicions were not aroused.

This is correct. It would be incorrect to write this sentence in this way:

> He had seen the accused man at the scene, he testified, but his suspicions had not been aroused.

The reason is that the words "he testified" are parenthetical and are not, in this case, those that govern the tense sequence of the other parts of the sentence. In the first case the facts asserted by the witness are clauses, and the tenses are governed by "he testified." In the second case, they are not clauses and are not governed by the parenthetical "he testified."

The normal sequence has one exception. When the fact set forth in the clause is permanently true, the tense of the clause is not governed by the main verb. For example, one says:

He said that the world is round (not was round).

In keeping the proper relation between the main verb and subordinate verb forms, an infinitive construction should have the present tense unless it represents action prior to that of the governing verb. It is incorrect to write:

It was unfortunate for him to have testified that he had seen the accused man at the scene.

It should read:

It was unfortunate for him to testify that he had seen the accused man at the scene.

A common mistake is to use a present participle in conjunction with a verb in the past tense. Here is an example:

Falling four stories and crashing through a skylight, John Jones, a painter, was saved from serious injury yesterday when he landed on a stack of books.

It should read:

Having fallen four stories and (having) crashed through a skylight, John Jones, a painter, was saved from serious injury yesterday when he landed on a stack of books.

False Passive or "Was Given" Construction. The subject in the active form of a sentence represents the actor, and the object, the receiver of the action; also, when the active form is changed to the passive, the receiver of the action becomes the subject, and the actor, if expressed, is represented as the object of a preposition. When a sentence in the active form contains both a direct and an indirect object, mistakes often are made in giving the passive construction. Frequently the indirect object in the active form is used as the subject in the passive form, but this makes an incorrect construction known as the false passive. Note these sentences. Active: *They gave him their heartfelt thanks for his trouble.* False passive: *He was given their heartfelt thanks for his trouble.* True passive: *Their heartfelt thanks were given to him for his trouble.* The first sentence contains both a direct and an indirect object. The direct object is the noun *thanks* and the indirect object is the pronoun *him.* In the second sentence it will be observed that the subject is represented by the word that is the indirect object in the active form of the sentence, and the predicate verb, which is passive, seems to be followed by an object. The third sentence shows the true passive form.

Pronouns and Antecedents. The copy editor should be vigilant to eliminate the pronoun "it" from copy, because the word almost always leaves the intent ambiguous. When it is necessary for clarity to repeat a subject, repeat or rephrase the sentence. Likewise, when several persons are mentioned in one sentence, the pronouns "he" and "she" should be avoided unless it is unmistakable what subject is intended. However, if the meaning is clear, the copy editor should not hesitate to strike out a noun and write in a pronoun when the repetition of the noun makes the sentence awkward. Note the ambiguity of pronouns in the following:

After the Governor and the Lieutenant-Governor had conferred for two hours concerning the advisability of levying additional taxes to balance the budget, *he* announced that a decision would be made within a week.

When the questioning of the witness had been completed, it was said at the District Attorney's office that the case would be laid before the grand jury next week only if *it* could be speeded.

TYPOGRAPHICAL STYLE

Every newspaper of standing has its own style for the spelling of many words, for abbreviations and for capitalization, and also special rules governing the quotation of titles of books, plays, songs, etc.

Some examples of variation of spelling are the following:

dominos	dominoes	vendor	vender
clue	clew	referenda	referendums
buses	busses	criticize	criticise
catalogue	catalog	controller	comptroller
entrust	intrust	anesthetic	anaesthetic
gayety	gaiety	ax	axe
gray	grey	calibre	caliber
guarantee	guaranty	closure	cloture
disk	disc	manoeuvre	maneuver
furor	furore	pretense	pretence
gibe	jibe	Tokio	Tokyo
grip	grippe	theatre	theater
plow	plough	glamour	glamor

There are wide differences in capitalization also. Most newspapers capitalize "President" when it stands alone and refers to the President of the United States; and all other titles when they stand alone and refer to a particular man, such as "the Governor," "the Mayor," and "the Senator" (but "the governors," "the mayors" and "the senators"). Street is capitalized when it refers to Wall Street, but some newspapers lower-case the "s" when street is part of an address.

Concerning abbreviations, it should be noted that some occur in headlines, where brevity is essential, but are not permitted in copy. Some of those permitted in copy are "Gov." for Governor, when followed by the name; "Col." for colonel (and most other military titles when followed by the name); but not "Pres." for President, nor "Sen." for Senator, even in headlines. It is permitted to abbreviate long names of organizations, such as Y.M.C.A., W.C.T.U. and I.C.C., but this practice is restricted to organizations whose names are thoroughly familiar to readers.

Some newspapers quote the titles of books, plays, songs and pictures; others do not. Still others quote some, but not all. The stylebook of the newspaper in the only guide in these cases and the copy editor should be familiar with its contents.

ERRORS OF FACT

The constant effort of the newspaper is to detect and to correct or eliminate errors of fact. To this end the copy and the proofs are examined by many persons; but on the copy editor falls the chief burden. Such mistakes are most frequent in dates, locations, and in the characterization or description of past events.

A distinction should be made between current events and those that are a matter of record. In the present, the facts of a situation may not be fully established. For example, the newspaper may print a story, based on the most accurate information available at the moment, saying that the victim of a murder was shot at Avenue X and Fifteenth Street. The following day, the case having been further clarified, the story may say that the victim was shot in his apartment at Avenue A and Sixtieth Street, and thrown into the street at the place where he was found. Such variation as this cannot be considered in the same light as in cases where the facts are fully known and recorded. This does not mean, however, that every effort should not be made to establish the truth of the statements in every story, no matter how minor it may appear in relation to other news. Serious consequences may follow from the printing of an incorrect name or address.

In past events, however, the facts are a matter of record. In the following illustrations several mistakes are made, any one of which might occur in a news story:

The disaster recalled the sinking of the German steamship Vestris on Dec. 12, 1928, 240 miles off the Virginia Capes, in which 110 lives were lost.

The liner made the westward crossing in 4 days 23 hours 6 minutes, only three hours behind the record set by the Europa in March, 1929.

Every fact and figure in these examples should be suspected by the copy editor and checked. After reference to an almanac containing records such as these or to the "morgue" clippings, he would edit the sentences as follows:

The disaster recalled the sinking of the British steamship Vestris on Nov. 12, 1928, 240 miles off the Virginia Capes, in which 110 lives were lost.

The liner made the westward crossing in 4 days 23 hours 6 minutes, only six hours behind the record set by the Europa in March, 1930.

The facts of a story must be consistent. If those in one paragraph contradict or cast doubt upon those in another paragraph, a change must be made in one case or the other. If the route of a robber's flight is described in one part of the story, he cannot be permitted to flee by any other route in another part of the story. Should the lead of the story say that the Mayor denounced waste in the city departments, the language of his statement must be, in fact, denunciatory. If he mildly criticizes only or suggests reforms, the lead must so describe his action. Each news story is a problem in clear, logical presentation.

Here is an example of an inconsistent lead:

Angered by criticism of "extravagance" in the city government, Mayor Blank denounced waste of the taxpayers' money before the city council yesterday and demanded that retrenchments be made "all along the line." He warned the heads of departments that 25 per cent reductions should be made in requests for funds in the next budget and that if drastic cuts were not made he might discover ways to make them. The Mayor spoke heatedly for twenty minutes and left the meeting abruptly. Action on several important measures had been on the calendar, but all were put over until the next session on Tuesday.

"I have heard much criticism of the cost of the government of the city," said the Mayor. "This criticism must be stopped by efforts to reduce expenditures all along the line. The President of the Board of Trade declares that, with a little effort, slashes of as much as 25 per cent can be made in the next budget. Perhaps it can be done. If you cannot do it, I may find ways to do it. If we fail, we can let our critics point the way.

"The taxpayers' money must not be wasted. Every dollar of it must be spent carefully and a dollar's worth of service obtained for it. But I am tired of continual attacks on this administration by persons who do not realize the mounting cost of every city department."

Such misrepresentation as is contained in the phrases "denounced waste" and "demanded retrenchments" might easily occur if an attempt is made to "sensationalize" the story. In the foregoing, the Mayor's words can certainly be interpreted as a warning and as a retort to his critics, but no more. The copy editor must soften the terms used to bring the lead into conformity with the quoted statement.

THE LEAD

The copy editor must know how to construct a story and must understand the importance of making the lead or introduction attract the attention of the reader.

There are two kinds of leads: one which puts the climax first, summarizing the important facts in the first few paragraphs; and the "delayed" lead, or feature-story lead, that works up to the climax later in the story. The first kind is the more common; it tells the news immediately and forcefully. The second, reserved for special types of stories, sets the mood and reaches the news point at a later stage.

This lead illustrates the direct method:

Tears, fainting spells and charges of "backbiting" and "politics" marked the final judgments on the show prizes of the thirtieth annual show of the Atlantic Cat Club yesterday. Although the judges reached quick decisions for most of the eight prizes awarded, a three-hour discussion and the services of a series of referees were required to settle whether a black cat with green eyes or a red cat of unknown parentage deserved the title of best novice and the accompanying $2.50 prize.

Here is a delayed, or feature-story, lead: [1]

Up six flights of stairs at 129 East Ninety-seventh Street, turn right in the gloomy hall and ring the bell on John Costen's door. You hear the soft, brushing movement of a hand on the inside panel, a fumbling on the knob and the door opens. John Costen has been blind for years.

But he was cheerful last night. Something like animation brightened the sightless gray eyes as he told about Dick, who swallowed the poker. Dick is his pet collie. Spends hours with him at the news stand on the northeast corner of Lexington Avenue and Ninety-sixth Street. Dick will be back from the hospital today.

"Best dog in the world," said Costen, "but maybe a little too active. He's only a year old, you see. Two weeks ago he was playing around here in the kitchen. I couldn't see him, of course. He reaches up and grabs the stove poker in his mouth and the handle comes off. A wire at the end of it got caught in Dick's tongue and, trying to get rid of that, he kept swallowing more and more of the handle."

One of the neighbors rushed Dick to a veterinarian in Yorkville, but he could not help. And there was the collie with a piece of iron six inches long and one inch around in his innards. He was taken to the Ellen Prince Speyer Hospital for Animals.

"They took an X-ray picture of him right away," Costen said, "and a friend of mine said it looked pretty bad, but Dr. Meyer, the veterinarian, gave Dick ether, opened Dick up, got the poker out and sewed him up again. He tells me he's as good as ever, and I'm going down today to get him."

[1] By the late Meyer Berger of *The New York Times.*

Making certain that the facts in the lead are correct and that the construction is right constitute more than half the task of copy editing. In the case of the direct news lead, the questions who or what, where, when and why or how, must be answered. If the location of the news event is the most striking, it must come first; if the "who" or "what" is the news point, the lead must be shaped so that that fact is the most prominently displayed. Every opening word is important. The word "the" should be used as little as possible in beginning a story, but it is not necessary to strain language or torture sentence structure to avoid it. To prevent using the word "the" as the opening word of a story, the participial clause was invented; but the method has been much abused.

An example of the "who" lead follows:

CHICAGO, Jan. 6—Julius Rosenwald, merchant and philanthropist, died in his sleep this afternoon at 2:55 o'clock at the age of 69. His wife and his five children were at the bedside as Dr. Herbert Pollock, attending physician, announced that Mr. Rosenwald was dead.

The following illustrates the "what" lead:

ALBANY, Jan. 5—Quotations from the Bible may be read in the public schools of New York City, the Court of Appeals ruled today when it affirmed the action of the lower court in dismissing the appeal of Joseph Lewis, President of the Freethinkers of America, who sought to prevent such reading. The court avoided any reference to the religious aspect of the case.

Here is a "where" lead:

The eighty-sixth floor of the Empire State Building, a thousand feet above Fifth Avenue, was the scene yesterday of an encounter between a city slicker and a country symbol. With scores of watchers on the observation platform, an English sparrow engaged in battle a praying mantis, blown New York-ward from its New Jersey habitat.

This is a "why" or "how" lead:

NORTH ARLINGTON, N.J., Jan. 5—A pair of carrier pigeons that Harvard Johnson and Paul Dolce, 16-year-old high school boys, took with them when they ran away from their homes on Wesley Place at 6 A.M. yesterday, so their messages to their parents could not be traced, caused their capture today.

The "when" lead is illustrated in the following:

During the noon hour when the crowds are greatest, Fifth Avenue and Forty-second Street—the hub of the city's midtown shopping center—was a scene of turmoil yesterday when a detective of the pickpocket squad fired five shots into the air to halt a man charged with having stolen $132 worth of neckties from a nearby shop.

If it is necessary to give authority to the story, the responsibility should be fixed at once. If the person making a statement is important, that is a vital point in the story and his name should appear as quickly as possible. Often a story is a story merely on account of the person or persons involved in it. A good rule for the copy editor is to let every man assume responsibility for his own statements or actions. It is not necessary for the newspaper to do so.

Here is illustrated the wrong way to write a story, in which responsibility should have been fixed at once and the authority cited:

The city's policy toward relief for the unemployed was condemned as "political" and as seeking to use public money to strengthen the hold of one party on the voters at a luncheon yesterday of the Southside Chamber of Commerce. After a strong plea had been made for an inquiry into the distribution and use of the $3,000,000 fund to aid the destitute through the Winter, a resolution was adopted demanding that the Mayor instruct the City Controller to investigate immediately and to report promptly.

The attack was made by James A. Osgood, banker, who was the chairman of the campaign to raise private funds to supply jobs to 10,000 heads of families. He has long been an intimate friend of the

Mayor and has previously supported the city's activities to relieve distress.

The following illustrates the proper method:

James A. Osgood, banker, who was chairman of the campaign to raise private funds to supply jobs to 10,000 heads of families, and who has long been an intimate friend of the Mayor, condemned yesterday the city's policy toward relief for the unemployed as "political" and as seeking to use public money to strengthen the hold of one party on the voters. The attack was made at a luncheon of the Southside Chamber of Commerce.

After Mr. Osgood had made a strong plea for an inquiry into the distribution and use of the $3,000,000 fund to aid the destitute through the Winter, the Chamber adopted a resolution demanding that the Mayor instruct the City Controller to investigate immediately and to report promptly.

A point to be remembered about leads is that the lead is not always restricted to one sentence and may be more than one paragraph.

THE DEVELOPMENT

When the lead is satisfactory, the development of the rest of the story is comparatively simple. The reporter or copy editor should make sure that the narrative, exposition or description develops logically or naturally. In the case of the direct news lead, in which the story is summarized or the main point emphasized a common practice is to return at once to the time when the story naturally starts and tell the events in the order in which they happened. Another method is to relate the occurrences in the order of their importance, rather than in sequence, but it requires more ingenuity to insure a smooth development. Skill in transition is required to avoid a jerky effect.

The "sequence" method of developing a news story after the lead is illustrated thus:

Surprised and overpowered by hold-up men they had been sent to capture, two detectives of the Second Avenue Station faced departmental charges last night because they had allowed themselves to be robbed of their revolvers and bound with other victims at Second Avenue and Third Street.

A robbery there Monday night, carried out with three score policemen in the vicinity, was kept secret by the police until yesterday morning. Then it became known that three gunmen had escaped from the offices of the XYZ Company with $2,000 and that the two policemen who had started out in the role of captors had become captives.

One of the men was Detective A. B. Jones, a veteran of the force, and the other was Detective R. A. Smith, who has been commended for arresting armed robbers.

At about 10 o'clock Monday night, according to F. O. Adams, manager of the company, he had taken the day's receipts of $2,000 from the safe, placed them in his pocket and was preparing to go home when three men entered. When he attempted to fight them one intruder struck Adams three times on the head with the butt of a pistol. Once inside, each of them drew a second pistol and rounded up two drivers who were on the premises.

Adams did not know that detectives had been called but he learned later that the thieves had failed to notice the presence of a night watchman, who telephoned for the police.

The robbers searched Adams, found the $2,000 and then ordered him to open the safe. Then a knock sounded on the door.

"One of the robbers opened the door and said, 'Come right in gentlemen,'" said Adams. "Smith came in first and Jones right after him. Neither one had his revolver drawn. Then the robbers ordered the detectives . . ."

In this example the development of the story begins with the phrase "at about 10 o'clock Monday night" and continues chronologically to give the details.

The development of facts in the order of their importance is more difficult as this illustration shows:

[1] WASHINGTON, March 31—First hearings on the President's Federal securities measure went swiftly forward today in House and Senate committees, developing some difference of opinion and bringing out testimony that of $50,000,000,000 in securities

floated in this country in the last thirteen years half had proved either "worthless or undesirable."

[2] Chairman X of the Interstate and Foreign Commerce Committee of the House, in which lengthy testimony was taken today, said that hearings would end Monday noon at the latest and possibly tomorrow.

[3] The Senate Banking and Currency Committee, which held a short hearing today, indicated that it would await action by the House, which is expected to come not later than the middle of next week.

[4] The conflict of opinion arose among Congressional leaders over just what securities the pending act would apply to. Senator Y, the Democratic leader, said that "if you don't apply the law to existing securities you lose 90 per cent of the value of the law," and it was his opinion that the measure would be made to apply to all outstanding issues.

[5] This was in sharp disagreement, however, with the views of the authors of the measure, including a former chairman of the Federal Trade Commission, and a representative of the Attorney General.

[6] They told the House committee that the law could apply only to flotations hereafter made or to securities which have already been authorized but not advertised or offered for sale to the public before the effective date of the new act.

[7] House Democratic leaders are preparing to make a determined stand for the securities measure, this determination being strengthened by intimations that some classes of issuers would seek to have themselves exempted from the "pitiless publicity" requirements of the measure.

[8] While they laid plans for swift action on the first step of the President's permanent program of protection for investors and depositors, the two other steps, to establish better supervision of the stock and commodity exchanges and eliminate unethical and unsafe banking practices, continued in abeyance pending action on the securities bill.

[9] Informal consideration of these subjects was going forward, however, both in official and business circles. A special committee of the Chamber of Commerce of the United States recommended in a report a single, unified commercial banking system for the country. The report suggested that every commercial bank, as distinguished from an investment institution, should ultimately be part of the Federal Reserve System.

[10] Sponsors of the securities act had not been informed tonight how many types of security issuers would seek to avoid its provisions. It was reported that railroad companies would oppose vigorously their inclusion in the part of the measure which compels detailed information about the issuer in any advertisement of a security flotation.

[11] An appeal was made openly to the House Committee to exempt building and loan associations from the requirement for registration of every security issue. This plea was made on the basis that such registration would work great inconvenience to many mutual building and loan societies, while the fee would work financial hardship.

[12] The railroad companies are not included among the issuers required by the act to register detailed information with the Federal Trade Commission, since their securities must be passed upon under present law by the Interstate Commerce Commission.

[13] But the exemptions to railroad companies are not repeated under the section providing for information that must be set forth if a stock issue is advertised to the public.

[14] Under that provision the railroads, if they advertised a stock or bond issue or if one were advertised for them by an investment house, would have to set forth an account of the whole transaction, including the fees to be paid to the bankers for handling the loan, the name of the underwriting syndicate, the capital structure of the railroad, including its assets and liabilities, and its profits and losses during the year just preceding the offering.

[15] Representative Z of New York, former chairman of the commerce committee and an authority on the railroad problem, insisted that jurisdiction over flotations of the carrier companies should be left entirely to the Interstate Commerce Commission, as at present.

[16] The House committee spent the greater part of the day listening to an explanation of the bill by the former chairman of the F.T.C., who took it up section by section, giving the history and the purpose of each and discussing with members the feasibility or desirability of changes here and there in the text.

[17] Out of it all came the clear indication that the framers of the measure as well as the Democrats of the committee proposed to stand by it practically as written. They had already concluded that the bill was virtually "airtight."

[18] Questions from the Republican side left an inference that an attempt would be made to make the bill more specific as to

the control of the Federal Trade Commission over the flotation of foreign securities in the United States.

[19] Under the terms of the bill the American underwriting syndicate or agent of a foreign government or industrial enterprise is compelled to register any proposed issue along with the information required. The only veto power the commission would have would be to revoke the registration and thus outlaw the issue.

[20] Representative XY of New Jersey insisted that the commission should have authority to stop foreign flotations without subterfuge.

[21] The witness answered that blunt action of that nature might offend sensitive governments to the point that they would construe it as an unfriendly act. He related that the State Department had practically such authority all along but hesitated to use it on that account.

[22] The chief of the Foreign Service Division of the Department of Commerce said that the State Department had been "very reluctant" to concern itself with foreign stock issues because of the lack of specific law on the subject. He said that under the pending act the Federal Trade Commission could discuss any particular foreign issue with the Cabinet officers involved and with representatives of the foreign power, and, on the basis of facts developed, ask the borrowing government to withdraw its issue if undesirable or of doubtful worth.

[23] "If the government in question should persist in its offering and refuse to withdraw its security issue, then the Federal Trade Commission could revoke its registration and no offense legitimately could be taken," he said.

[24] Under questioning of Mr. XY, he estimated that $12,000,-000,000 in foreign securities, both governmental and private, had been issued in this country. He declined to estimate how many had gone into default, saying simply that a "very substantial portion" had either "gone bad" or deteriorated to the point of worthlessness.

[25] He was also authority for the estimate that $50,000,000,000 in securities had been floated in the United States in thirteen years, and that about half of them had proved undesirable or worthless.

[26] "This law is designed to stop that sort of business," he said.

[27] The former F.T.C. chairman explained in his testimony that the bill was based on the theory that adequate public information about security issues would amply protect the public.

[28] "We can't protect fools," he said, "but we can give in-

vestors every reasonable opportunity to obtain information through the Federal Trade Commission on securities offered for sale."

[29] He referred frequently to the British securities act, from which many of the bill's ideas were taken, and to the Martin act of New York State, from which the language was copied.

[30] He also referred often to a copy of the book of Associate Justice Brandeis of the Supreme Court on "Other People's Money."

[31] A model advertisement for stock issues under the proposed law was lifted bodily from this book and placed in the record.

[32] The Attorney General's representative, declared that the bill's purpose could be summed up in the words: "Pitiless publicity of all facts of which purchasers of securities should be informed."

This story merits the close reading and analysis of the student of journalism. Not only is a long and complicated story well developed as to the lead and subsequent structure, but it also shows excellent condensation of the mass of testimony taken before the House committee. It will be noted that the first three paragraphs constitute the lead, stating the high lights of the story—that hearings went forward swiftly on the securities measure, that differences of opinion developed, that testimony was given that half the huge total of securities floated in this country in thirteen years was of doubtful value—and making clear the status of the bill in Congress. The development of the story begins with paragraph 4 with the transition words "the difference of opinion arose" which, reiterating a phrase in paragraph 1 in almost identical words, shows that that phase of the lead is to be dealt with. Paragraphs 5 and 6 elaborate this, each paragraph developing smoothly from the preceding one because of the transition words "this was in sharp disagreement" and "they told the House committee." Paragraph 7 introduces two new subjects—the Democratic leaders' attitude and the demand for exemptions from the provisions of the bill —which can be expected to come up again later in detail.

Paragraph 8 brings in still another subject that is almost

parenthetical—the status of other bills relating to the same situation—but it is done smoothly with the clause "while they laid plans for swift action." Paragraph 9 elaborates paragraph 8 and that phase of the story is then completed.

Paragraph 10 begins the development of the "exemption phase" of the story, first stated in paragraph 7, and is also elaboration of the lead point of "difference of opinion." Paragraphs 11, 12, 13, 14 and 15 continue and complete this subject. Paragraph 16 gives in detail the hearing before the House committee, one of the lead points, and recurs to paragraph 5 where the former F.T.C. chairman is mentioned as a witness. Paragraph 17, worked in smoothly with the clause "out of it all came the clear indication," elaborates and explains paragraph 7. Paragraph 18, elaborated in paragraphs 19, 20 and 21, refers inferentially to the lead point concerning worthless securities, a phase of the story that is given in full detail in paragraphs 22, 23, 24, 25, and 26. The former trade commission officials' testimony is dealt with in paragraphs 27, 28, 29, 30 and 31. Paragraph 32 touches on the testimony of the Attorney General's aide, mentioned specifically in paragraph 5.

To recapitulate briefly, three points were stated in the lead, necessitating their elaboration and substantiation in the development in the order of importance. The difference of opinion was dealt with first, then the detail of the hearing bringing out various phases of the differences, and then the testimony concerning worthless securities. It is beside the point whether there is agreement on this order of news values; the writer so rated them and developed his story accordingly. It may be of interest to note that the headline for this story was "Securities Hearing Divides Leaders; Measure Is Rushed."

While transition sentences or phrases are less common in newspaper writing than elsewhere, they preserve the unity of the story. This is particularly true, as in the foregoing case, when one point in the lead has been amplified and another is to be taken up. Transition phrases frequently seen are "earlier in the day," "just before his arrival" and "prior to this development." The word "meanwhile" or the phrase "in the meantime" serve also for transition when the story turns to events that happened simultaneously with those previously related.

In the lead, the striking points have been summarized only. In the development, these points must be amplified but not repeated as matters of new fact. If the copy editor discovers that they are not mentioned again, there is something wrong with the development, or the inclusion of those points in the lead is questionable. Every fact in the lead must be supported later in detail; or it must be dealt with to the extent of giving enough background facts to show why it is important.

Such a case as this occurs often. A man mentioned as a candidate for office may, in the course of an otherwise routine speech, indicate that he will enter the contest or that he will not. This fact alone makes a story and is, of course, the lead. But the bald statement cannot stand alone. The background must be told by the reporter or supplied by a rewrite man or the copy editor to show the significance of the action. The statement is lifted from its context to construct the news story properly, but substance must be given to it by showing why it is important.

In recent years there has been a new look at news writing in general and at news leads in particular. It is felt no longer that the five W's must be set forth at once or completely. In the interest of clear and simple writing it is now considered better to state the main point tersely, readably and forcefully, letting the contributory facts follow in a natural development of the story. This is a step in the direction of informing the reader faster. To insure his attention and comprehension, one idea to one sentence is regarded as essential. And the shorter the sentence the better.

Involved also is the need to give background and essential interpretation to inform the reader fully. This new element of reporting deserves some discussion. Fundamentally, a fact is a physical thing—a fire, an automobile crash, a speech, a convention—which are events that can be recorded in a straightforward account.

But consider the instance of Senator Jones, a member of the Senate Foreign Relations Committee, who makes a speech on the floor of the Senate giving his views of the current crisis and his proposals for meeting it. The only facts are that he spoke and that he made proposals which will be quoted at the necessary length and the text printed if warranted by his importance and the nature of his solution. This would meet the old, and largely continuing, formula of news writing.

Is this enough? The crisis Senator Jones is dealing with might be a crucial episode in United States relations with a foreign power and to report only his remarks might leave the reader in the dark. He is not fully informed and certainly not enlightened.

The speech must be set in a background of the whole complex picture of foreign relations at the moment, the position of this and other countries, how their policies can be affected by the views of this important official, what Washington reaction and that of other capitals is or might be.

To meet current requirements of news writing, it probably would be necessary to employ the time-honored "informed sources," "a spokesman," "observers," "persons close to the Secretary" and the like.

There is a danger here to the accepted principle that news

should be gathered and published objectively. There is a thin line between interpretation and opinion. Great skill in phrasing is required to add perspective and depth to a set of facts without expressing or indicating a point of view.

Nevertheless these goals—simplicity, clarity, depth and perspective—are increasingly needed as local, national and foreign situations become more complex. There is a growing need also to inform newspaper readers quickly because of the keen competition for a share of their leisure time.

THE SENTENCE

The short simple sentence is the most effective for news writing. As in every other kind of writing, however, there must be variety. A common misconception among beginners is that the first sentence must contain the answers to the questions who or what, where, when and why or how. This leads invariably to an involved sentence structure that is neither clear nor effective. The copy editor should break up long sentences, even though they may be clear. The effect of a sentence is lost if a dozen lines of type must be read before the end is reached.

The involved one-sentence lead is illustrated thus:

> Returning to the city yesterday from a two-week vacation in the South, Governor Anderson issued a statement of defiance to his opponents, who, according to reports in political circles, are planning to "put him in a hole" over the tax measure that is expected to be drafted next week at a meeting of the Republican leaders, by throwing upon the Executive the burden of seeking new sources of revenue and forcing him to shoulder the political consequences of what may prove to be an unpopular program, and declared that he was ready for a fight to the finish on the legislative measures that he considered to be of paramount importance at this session.

A better way to write the lead is:

> Returning to the city yesterday from a two-week vacation in the South, Governor Anderson issued a statement of defiance to his op-

ponents and declared that he was ready for a fight to the finish on the legislative measures that he considered to be of paramount importance at this session.

The Republicans, according to reports in political circles, are planning to "put him in a hole" over the tax measure that is expected to be drafted next week at a meeting of the Republican leaders. They plan to throw upon the Executive the burden of seeking new sources of revenue and force him to shoulder the political consequences of what may prove to be an unpopular program.

Paragraphing is not haphazard and usually not an arbitrary breaking up of the story into units for regular type display. Paragraphing, like sentence structure, must follow the rules of rhetoric. For an extended discussion, the grammars should be consulted. In general, a paragraph indicates to the reader that a new subject or a new phase of the same subject is to be taken up. Everything relating to the same phase of the news story should, if possible, be in the same paragraph, although long paragraphs are as much to be avoided as long sentences.

For emphasis a separate paragraph may be made arbitrarily, and direct quotations usually should be paragraphed.

The following is an example of bad paragraphing:

Mr. X said that as soon as the announcement was made that his expedition was ready to leave, he was flooded with applications from women as well as from men.

One woman writer confided that she hoped to find with the expedition "occult and stirring" material for a new book.

Another applied for the post of private secretary, but said that if that post were filled she would like to create "a home atmosphere" for the explorers in the wastes of Asia.

Mr. X was skeptical about the possibilities for "home atmosphere" in a desert where sandstorms continued for weeks, and where the proportion of bandits to the number on the expedition was about 300 to 1.

Mr. X found China "foggy with bandits" but not of the New York variety.

The Chinese bandit, he said, cannot shoot, and does not want to kill a foreigner if he can help it.

If paragraphed in the following manner, the unity of thought is retained:

Mr. X said that as soon as the announcement was made that his expedition was ready to leave, he was flooded with applications from women as well as from men.

One woman writer confided that she hoped to find with the expedition "occult and stirring" material for a new book. Another applied for the post of private secretary, but said that if that post were filled she would like to create "a home atmosphere" for the explorers in the wastes of Asia. Mr. X was skeptical about the possibilities for "home atmosphere" in a desert where sandstorms continued for weeks, and where the proportion of bandits to the number on the expedition was about 300 to 1.

Mr. X found China "foggy with bandits," but not of the New York variety. The Chinese bandit, he said, cannot shoot and does not want to kill a foreigner if he can help it.

TONING DOWN AND BRIGHTENING UP

The copy editor frequently hears the order, "tone it down." This means that the story has been phrased too strongly or that the perspective is wrong. Often the toning-down process can be accomplished merely by eliminating adjectives, changing strong verbs to milder ones and striking out words that characterize or describe in a manner that is distasteful. The order "clean it up" has a similar intent, but refers usually to crime or similar stories that are told in too explicit language. Good taste often is involved and it is the copy editor's task to eliminate offensive phases of the story. This kind of editing does not entail the suppression of facts; it merely requires that the story be told in polite language.

Here is a story that should be toned down:

JERSEY CITY, N.J., Jan. 12—Several neighbors saw Gustaf A. Petersen in his backyard at 101 Twenty-fifth Street, Union City, today sharpening a knife on a whetstone. At intervals Petersen stopped to examine the knife, which had a six-inch blade and was of a type used by shoemakers.

Mrs. William Orr, whose kitchen window looks out over Petersen's yard, saw him examine the knife for the fourth or fifth time. Then, she told the police, she saw him smile as if pleased, raise the knife and slash his throat. She shouted for help. Several men climbed over fences to reach Petersen. He was taken to the North Hudson Hospital in Weehawken but he was dead on arrival there.

Petersen was 51 years old and was a ship's carpenter.

The story may be edited as follows to remove the gruesome features:

JERSEY CITY, N.J., Jan. 12—Gustaf A. Petersen, 51 years old, a ship's carpenter, committed suicide in his backyard at 101 Twenty-fifth Street, Union City, today by slashing his throat with a knife. Mrs. William Orr, whose kitchen window overlooks Petersen's yard, saw his act and summoned help. Several neighbors told the police that they had seen Petersen in his yard whetting the knife, which had a six-inch blade and was of the type used by shoemakers.

"Brightening up" a story requires the judicious use of adjectives or of colorful or active verbs, or the "lifting" of a phrase or sentence from the detail of the story to the lead, helping to transform the whole from a dull account into an interesting one.

Examine the following statistical story to see what can be done with it to make it of interest to readers.

OSSINING, N.Y., Jan. 3—Sing Sing attachés disclosed today that a total of 1,740 lawbreakers were received at the prison last year, 1,038 were transferred by the warden to up-State prisons and that the prison population at the end of the year was more than 2,400 men and one woman.

Besides those transferred the total number of convicts was reduced by 555, 32 of whom died and 523 of whom were discharged. Four hundred and eighty were paroled; 10 were pardoned by the Governor: 9 won reversals of their convictions; certificates of reasonable doubt were granted to 2 and 14 were released for resentencing. Only 8 of those discharged from the prison served their maximum terms.

It probably will be agreed that only one fact strikes the eye as being of general interest and that the last one: that "only eight served their maximum terms." The problem then is to make that fact the lead. It appears to be a rewrite man's work, but it can be edited by clipping the story in two between the paragraphs, writing a paragraph lead, editing the second paragraph to read smoothly from the new lead and editing the old lead to go at the end. This is how it will look:

OSSINING, N.Y., Jan. 3—Only eight of 523 prisoners discharged from Sing Sing prison in 1931 served their maximum terms, it was disclosed at the prison today.

The total number of convicts was reduced by 32 deaths. Of the 523 discharged, 480 were paroled; 10 were pardoned by the Governor; 9 won reversals of their convictions; certificates of reasonable doubt were granted to 2 and 14 were released for resentencing.

During the year 1,740 lawbreakers were received at the prison and 1,038 were transferred by the warden to up-State prisons. The prison population at the end of the year was more than 2,400 men and one woman.

TRIMMING, CUTTING, AND BOILING DOWN

The copy editor frequently must shorten a story to fit into a space indicated, or to enable the editor in charge to keep within his total space allotment. This entails trimming, cutting, and boiling down, which are similar processes but which vary in degree.

Trimming is a general tightening up of the story, chiefly by eliminating superfluous words and replacing loose phrases with single words that express the thought adequately. The following is an example of paragraphs that should be trimmed:

The Governor, upon whom the duty of finding the necessary funds to keep the State machinery moving devolves, will deal in detail with measures which he has formulated with this end in view, when his executive budget is presented to the law-making body next week. He has given little or no intimation as to what measure he will recommend to provide the necessary funds. It is the prevailing opinion among persons in his confidence, however, that he will resort to no new forms of taxation but will depend on increasing existing levies. It appears to be definitely known, however, by friends of the Governor that doubling of the present tax on gasoline will be asked.

While the Governor declared entirely unfounded reports that the State Treasury was nearly empty, he admitted that resort to short term borrowing might be necessary in order to provide funds for the administrative departments.

The Assembly Republicans met in caucus tonight for the purpose of designating their leaders.

Trimming will reduce these 163 words to 116, a saving of 47 words, or one-fourth of the space, thus:

The Governor, who must find the necessary funds to keep the State machinery moving, will deal in detail with revenue measures when his executive budget is presented next week. He has given little intimation what measure he will recommend. It is the opinion of persons in his confidence, however, that he will resort to no new forms of taxation but will depend on increasing existing levies. It appears definite that doubling of the tax on gasoline will be asked.

The Governor denied reports that the State Treasury was nearly empty, but admitted short term borrowing might be necessary to provide funds for the administrative departments.

The Assembly Republicans met in caucus tonight to designate their leaders.

Two phrases should be noted: "in order to," which can nearly always be shortened to "to"; and "for the purpose of," which also usually can be expressed simply by "to."

Boiling down is more drastic and is the process of close paring of all sentences and the sacrifice of minor facts. Here is a problem in boiling down:

Several women subway passengers, frightened by the lightning-like flashes of a short-circuit, had to be assisted last night from the B.M.T. tracks under Seventh Avenue to the street near Forty-ninth Street by an emergency exit, followed by 200 other passengers, in an accident that caused a traffic tie-up for twenty minutes. No one was injured.

The mishap occurred at 7:55 P.M. when a Brighton local train, headed north for Queens Plaza, was approaching the Forty-ninth Street station. A piece of equipment beneath one car came in contact with the third rail, causing the short circuit.

The train had sufficient momentum to carry it into the Forty-ninth Street station, where the engineer halted it to allow the passengers to be discharged. Soon after the train stopped, a north-bound Fourth Avenue local approached on the same tracks. The engineer of this train, seeing the Brighton local in the station, stopped his train short of the station platform. The vivid electric flashes, lighting up the tunnel, frightened some of the passengers of the Fourth Avenue local. In a few moments, however, the power was shut off, leaving the train stranded several hundred feet from the Forty-ninth Street station platform.

With the danger of the deadly third rail removed, the passengers on the crowded train were allowed to leave the cars. They scrambled to the tracks, picked their way through the darkness to the emergency exit, helping the more timid passengers as they went.

During the twenty minutes in which the power was off all north-bound local trains on the line were rerouted along the center tracks which run from Times Square and are used ordinarily for the shunting of express trains which end their runs at the Square.

Boiling down reduces the number of words from 285 to 165, a saving of 120 words, or two-fifths of the space formerly required, as follows:

Several women subway passengers, frightened by the flashes of a short-circuit caused when a piece of equipment struck the third rail, had to be assisted last night from the B.M.T. tracks under Seventh Avenue to the street near Forty-ninth Street by an emergency exit, followed by 200 other passengers. The accident tied up traffic for twenty minutes. No one was injured.

The mishap occurred at 7:55 P.M. when a north-bound Brighton local was approaching the Forty-ninth Street station. It had sufficient momentum to carry it into the station, where the passengers were discharged.

Soon afterward, a Fourth Avenue local approached on the same tracks. The engineer stopped his train short of the station. The vivid electric flashes frightened some passengers but soon the power was shut off, leaving the train stranded. With the danger of the third rail removed, the passengers were allowed to leave the cars to grope through darkness to the exit.

While the power was off all north-bound local trains were rerouted.

Cutting means the elimination of all but the most important facts, those without which there would be no story or an incomplete one. Often there is nothing left but the bare bones of a story with a shred or two of clothing. Many news stories can be so reduced without loss to the reader. Routine court stories, which must be published for one reason or another, can be cut to brief, unadorned recitals.

Here is a story to be cut:

New Yorkers are so accustomed to shouting at one another above the crash of steel and stone, the din of subways and noise of traffic that they shout over the dinner table in voices that are not musical but piercing and strident, Jack Robinson, the writer, told a radio audience yesterday afternoon over Station XYZ.

Mr. Robinson complained that even the exterior walls of buildings are sound boxes which hurl back noises into suffering ears, and as a remedy he suggested the use of acoustically treated surfacing.

Speaking under the auspices of the New York Noise Abatement Commission, Mr. Robinson told his listeners that the most offensive noises originate with such transit facilities as subway trains, brake-screeching automobiles and horn-honking taxicabs. A group of persons in a European restaurant and a group from a similar social background in a New York eating place, he went on, form a remarkable contrast.

"In Europe," he said, "the conversation is subdued, yet far more audible because it is more musical than with us. You can't expect the New Yorker to bring his voice down again during the lunch or dinner hour if all the rest of the day he must compete with the crash of steel and stone around him."

He added that our descendants will no doubt marvel that "we put up with the torture of riveting machines which are building a house next door, but will marvel much more that we endured so long without protest noises which were not temporary but part of our life from year's end to year's end."

When cut, the story looks like this:

New Yorkers are so accustomed to shouting at one another above the city's clamor that they shout over the dinner table in piercing and strident voices, Jack Robinson, the writer, told a radio audience yesterday afternoon over Station XYZ. He spoke under the auspices of the New York Noise Abatement Commission.

Mr. Robinson complained that even the exterior walls of buildings are sound boxes which hurl back noises and suggested the use of acoustically treated surfacing. He said that the more offensive noises originate with trolleys, subways, elevated trains, automobiles and taxicabs. Our descendants, he said, will marvel that we endured such din so long.

The voices of Europeans, he added, are musical and, while subdued, more audible.

By this method the story of 264 words has been reduced to 118 or to less than half. This drastic treatment depends wholly upon the space allotted to the story and is resorted to only in cases where the press of news is so great that much must be lost.

FAIRNESS, PUBLICITY, AND LIBEL

In any of these processes, care should be taken that no elimination of a fact leaves a wrong impression. Both sides to a dispute or lawsuit should have equal treatment. If the removal of a fact distorts the story in any respect, if a question is left in the mind, the fact should be retained.

As to fairness, the copy editor should make sure that every party to a controversy gets a hearing. If a man is accused, an effort should be made to include his comment in the same story in which the charges are published. Sometimes this effort is indicated only by a sentence saying that the accused man "was not reached for comment." This tends to show the impartiality of the newspaper. If no effort to obtain both sides of the story has been made, the copy editor should call the attention of the editor in charge to the failure to do so.

While trimming, cutting or boiling down, the copy editor should take special pains to remove words or names that give unwarranted publicity to persons or things, or that tend to advertise improperly stores or other places or goods of any kind.

He should also eliminate editorial opinion or any bias that tends, or might tend, to indicate an attitude or opinion by the newspaper or the copy editor himself. Some freedom is allowed in news stories that are written under a by-line, that is, signed by the writer, but this leeway is limited by the policy of the newspaper. For example, a political writer is permitted in a signed story to express, usually in a highly qualified manner, his views of the outcome of a campaign.

Libel is generally described as the publication of material that impeaches the honesty, integrity, virtue or reputation of a living person, thereby holding him up to public ridicule or contempt or causing him financial injury. It is not always possible to avoid printing some libelous statements, but if the newspaper is sued for damages, its defenses are three: (1) to prove that the defamatory statements were true; (2) to show that the statements were part of a court record or other official or public proceedings and therefore privileged; (3) to show that the publication was in good faith and without malice. This is not strictly a defense, but a plea in mitigation of damages.

The copy editor should remember that such phrases as "it was said," "it was alleged," and "according to the police," are no protection against a libel suit, but they tend to show a lack of malice and are therefore valuable. The questions "Is it true?" and "Is it privileged?" serve as a general rule of thumb that will solve many problems of the copy editor. He should, however, become familiar with the libel laws of his state and have more than a slight acquaintance with case histories.

The copy editor should be careful to avoid anonymous or

irresponsible statements. He should beware also of the "funny story" lest the persons named or indicated be made to appear ridiculous.

SUBHEADS

Stories of more than half-column in length are broken up by subheads. These are, in effect, small one-line headlines and should follow the rules for headlines; that is, to say something, not to be merely labels. They are set in body type but have a blacker face. The technical designation in some offices is "fflc" or "bflc," meaning "full face lower case," "black face lower case" or "bold face lower case." In other offices subheads are designated by letter or number. They should be placed about every quarter-column, but there should rarely be fewer than two. Practice varies as to where they should be placed, some newspapers requiring that they be inserted regularly for balance, and others requiring that they be placed at the natural "breaks" in the subject matter of the story.

The purpose of subheads is to interrupt long stretches of type that are unattractive to the reader's eye and to indicate the subject matter of the type appearing under them.

TYPE DISPLAYS

Unusual type displays often are employed by newspapers to emphasize leads or other parts of a news story. One method is to set the lead or other matter to be stressed in a type larger than the ordinary body type. For example, if the body type of the newspaper is seven point, the matter to be emphasized is set in eight point and, in unusual cases, in ten point. It is not uncommon also for this type to be set in black face to give added prominence.

The more common practice to display type is by indentations or hanging indentations. Texts and lists of names of various kinds are so displayed, especially if the names are accompanied by titles or other descriptions. Long lists of names, not followed by titles, usually are set in agate type in half-column measure to save space as well as to display them. Figures are displayed by setting them in tabular form, usually in agate type.

Still other methods to display type to emphasize reading matter are the one-column and two-column boxes. The one-column box is type set in one-column measure but ruled off in the newspaper to give a box effect. The two-column box, in addition to being boxed, is set in two-column measure and, by breaking up the regular one-column style, serves to attract attention.

The following show some of the more common ways of displaying special material.

The main points of a proposal, when summarized in a story or when printed in textual form, can be set in this way:

> . . . The recommendations of the committee, after a six-month study, for beautifying the lower part of the city and relieving traffic congestion which, in recent years, has become acute in that district, were:
>
> Razing of buildings on both sides of Second Street from Avenue X to Avenue Z and the widening of Second Street to eighty feet to eliminate the "bottle neck" which delays traffic and developing the street as a through-traffic artery to the bridges to the east.
>
> Razing of tenement structures on four blocks, bounded by Avenues V and X and Fourth and Sixth Streets, for the construction of a new municipal office building and with the eventual aim of developing the tract as a civic center and park area.

This method is the ordinary indentation, the copy being marked simply "indent."

A list of committee members, in which the names are followed by titles, would be set thus:

JOHN HAMMOND, President of the Board of Trade; in charge of the arrangements to welcome distinguished guests during the convention week.

GEORGE S. JONES, President of the Bank of Commerce; in charge of the program and leader of the round-table discussions on Wednesday.

Mrs. ALFRED O. GARDNER, Secretary of the Women's Voters' League; in charge of arrangements for women delegates.

The copy is marked, in this case, "agate hanging indent names caps."

A list of dead and injured would be set similarly, thus:

The Dead

JACKSON, FRANK D., 48 years old, of 203 Sanford Street; died of a fractured skull in City Hospital.

MORGAN, W. A., 36, of 889 Homestead Avenue; died of a fractured skull and internal injuries at General Hospital.

The Injured

MOLLOY, FRANCIS P., 21, of 12 East Avenue; fractured right arm and right leg, lacerations of the head and shoulders; in City Hospital.

The copy, as in the preceding illustration, is marked "agate hanging indent names caps." It is a general practice in such lists to put the surname first.

A long list of students, for example a graduating class, is set as follows:

College of Engineering

Albert A. Anderson	O. Karl Jaffer
A. McC. Blaines	James B. Jones
Andrew W. Bullard	F. O. Smith
John B. Butler	W. O. Waverley
F. F. Cooper	John S. Williamson
Arthur L. Hopper	

College of Architecture

Fred B. Bronsome	Lois A. Jones
Johnson Crittenden	T. M. Roberts
A. F. Farley	

The style is indicated by "agate half measure." The divisions are marked "fflc."

The copy editor is required to be familiar with all forms of type display employed by his newspaper and to indicate on the copy the style to be used in setting type, if the desired style is other than the usual body type.

SCISSORS AND PASTE

All newspaper copy is typewritten and is either double or triple spaced, the latter being the better because more room is provided for corrections. Triple space gives ample room for most editing, but there are times when several sentences must be interlined. Ordinarily this requires that copy be cut at that point, the necessary matter written on a separate sheet and pasted in at the proper place. The copy editor should not write up or down in the margins of the copy, since such editing causes difficulties for the compositor.

If paragraphs must be taken out at one place and inserted in another, scissors and paste should be used. Indicated transpositions are not possible in copy unless all of the transposed matter and the place to which it is to be shifted are on the same sheet. A paragraph can be made to precede or follow another by indicating lines if both begin and end on the same sheet of copy.

In some offices it is permitted to paste copy into a long continuous sheet for the convenience of the copy cutter, a composing room employee who cuts the copy into short lengths for convenient setting; but in most offices the pages should be no longer than the ordinary sheet of typewriting paper.

In the matter of neatness, the copy editor should write legibly. It is not necessary for him to write a fine hand; it may be schoolboyish, if it can be read. It is futile to cramp words into a small space, to save the trouble of cutting and pasting, if the interlined matter cannot be read easily. The copy must be intelligible to many persons besides the copy editor. The compositor must be able to read quickly and correctly; and the proofreader also. Copy badly put together and slovenly deletion marks or editing slow up the process of getting out a newspaper and increase the chances for error.

When the copy editor is in doubt about a point in a story, four courses are open to him. If the questioned fact is not vital, it may be deleted. This should be a last resort, however, not an easy way out of a difficulty. If the question can be cleared up by means of a reference book, it should be checked in that manner. If it can be checked only by reference to the reporter, he should be consulted. Questions of policy, taste or consistency usually are referred to the head of the desk for decision, and by him to higher editors if it becomes necessary.

HEADLINES

When the copy has been edited with attention to the foregoing suggestions, the copy editor's next task is to write a headline for the story. The headline, which is fully considered in the second division of this book, must first be accurate, not only in point of fact but also in spirit. Facts can be so placed in reference to one another that a meaning apart from the words themselves may be derived. The headline also should tell the whole story, or as much of it as space will permit, in a forceful and attractive way.

It has been noted that students of journalism concentrate on headline writing more than on the editing of copy. This is perhaps owing to the fact that headline writing is a challenge to their ingenuity and that headlines show to better advantage than editing. No error could be graver. If such a point of view carries over into newspaper work, the copy editor will be disillusioned speedily.

THE PROOF

A galley proof is taken of all matter that is set in type for the newspaper. These proofs are available to the copy editor and it is by means of them that he indicates to the composing room any changes that are to be made before the newspaper goes to press.

Major errors should be corrected in the proof but minor editing in proof is not approved. This should have been completed by the editor in the copy. He should keep in mind that the changing of one word in proof means that a whole line must be reset, since the linotype machine sets by line and not by word. The changing or deletion of one word at the beginning of a paragraph may require the resetting of the whole paragraph.

When the copy editor gets the first edition, it is his duty to read every story he has edited and every headline he has written, to detect any errors that may have been made in typesetting. Minor typographical mistakes are left to the proofreader, to avoid duplication of effort, but major errors should be corrected. The same limitations govern editing in the newspaper as apply to editing in the proof. Resetting of type is to be avoided if possible, but this consideration is not to stand in the way of necessary corrections. Errors in names should be corrected by the copy editor without relying on the proofreader to detect them. No effort is too great to insure that names are spelled correctly.

When corrections or changes are to be made in the newspaper, the story should be clipped out and pasted on copy paper. The page and column numbers are noted on the copy paper and the desired changes carefully indicated by lines drawn from the point in type where the error occurs to the copy paper, where the change can be shown clearly. Corrections should not be written on the newspaper page because of the danger of illegibility. A second reason for clipping out the story is that each correction is on a page of a size easily handled and the composing room is not forced to cope with a mass of paper of irregular shapes.

The copy editor is responsible for the correctness and appearance of every story that has passed through his hands. It is not enough for him to be sure that the copy and the headline leave the copy desk in perfect order; he must be sure that the one appears as he edited it and the other as he wrote it. He must detect mistakes made by the composing room. In other words, he must follow his stories from copy to print.

The importance of thoroughness cannot be overemphasized. Not only should the copy editor indicate every paragraph mark in the copy and make every deletion mark carefully, but he should also read the newspaper critically to assure himself that the story and its appearance are as perfect as it is possible to make them. Thus he assures the newspaper reader of a finished professional product.

4. MECHANICS OF COPY EDITING

THE SIGNS employed by the copy editor to indicate (in the copy itself, not in the margin as the proofreader does in proof) omissions, corrections or other directions to the compositor are commonly these:

The caret	ti repetion
or	would he said he appear

(This sign, indicating omission of words or letters or showing other interlined matter, is placed below the line while the interlined words or letters are placed above the line.)

Paragraph	L	or	¶
Capitalize	m		
Lower case	M		
Transpose	he yesterday said		
or	coulbe		
Strike out	repettition		
or	he said that he would go		

(The horizontal line is used also to delete sentences. When it is necessary to strike out several lines of copy, a line should be drawn from the end of the sentence preceding the deleted matter to the beginning of the sentence following as a convenience to the compositor. Every guide that can be given to facilitate his work should be given.)

Separate	hesaidthat	
Close up	h e sa id tha t	
Spell out	(45th) Street	
Contract	(One Hundred third) Street	
End mark	(////)	#

THE SLUG

Most stories have a name or designation called a slug. In some newspaper offices, only stories that require display headlines carry slugs; in others, all stories have them. There is a mechanical reason for this. If a story is short and the headline small, both the story and the headline can be set on the same linotype machine. Both are disposed of by one compositor in a single operation. If the story is long and the headline large, however, story and headline become separated in the composing room, the body type being set on one group of machines and the headline on another. The slug, then, becomes the guide of the make-up editors and the printers. It enables them to bring the proper headlines and stories together again.

The slug should be descriptive of the story; that is, if the story is about a suicide, the word "suicide" should appear as the slug or part of it. It is better for slugs to consist of two words, although brevity is desirable. "Girl Suicide," "Hotel Suicide" or "River Suicide" are better slugs than simply "Suicide." The use of two words helps to avoid confusion when there may be more than one suicide story in type for the same issue of the newspaper. Such words as "Policeman," "Building," "Broadway," "Harbor," are inadequate as slugs, because they give no clue to what the story is about. The following are better, since they convey an immediate idea of the kind of story: "Cop Shot," "Building Collapse," "Broadway Fire," "Harbor Fog."

For important stories that have many angles, the system of slugs is modified. If the general story is about a sea rescue, the general slug, and that of the lead story, would be "Rescue Lead." Related stories describing in detail phases of the rescue, would be slugged "Rescue-Survivors," "Rescue-Captain,"

"Rescue-Witness," "Rescue-List." All of these indicate what the stories are about; "Rescue" being, so to speak, the generic slug and the other designation the specific slug.

In some newspaper offices the slug carries through the whole process of printing several editions of the newspaper; in others the slug is "lost" after the first edition and in succeeding editions the story is designated by the headline or by part of it. In the latter case a story originally slugged "Harbor Fog" would become known by the top line of the display headline, which might be "Fog Ties Up Harbor."

HEAD TO COME

In the normal routine of the copy desk, story and headline are sent to the composing room together and no marks of instruction are required except the slug and the kind of headline required. When for any reason, however, it is necessary to rush copy to the composing room, stories may be edited and sent on, with the designation "Head to Come," or usually "H.T.K.," before the headline is written. The slug on the copy would be, for example, "Harbor Fog—H.T.K." This method makes it possible for the type to be set and the story made ready to put into the page form by the time the headline is written and set.

SECTIONAL STORIES

As the deadline for the first edition approaches, it is necessary for some stories to be sent in sections, or "takes." A take is two or three paragraphs of a story. In a case of this kind, the first take bears a slug such as "Harbor Fog," the kind of head that is to be written and the designation, "H.T.K." The entire slug, then, would be "Harbor Fog-C-H.T.K." The "C" represents the kind of head.[1] "More" is marked at the end of the first take, indicating to the composing room that there is more of the story to come.

The next take is slugged, "First Ad Harbor Fog" and "more" is marked at the end of the take. The next is slugged "Second Ad Harbor Fog" with "more" at the end of the take. If the next section is the last, it is slugged "Third and Last Ad Harbor Fog" and the end mark is placed at the end of that section. Sometimes the end is indicated by "End Third and Last Ad End Story" to insure that no mistake is made, but the end mark suffices. Thus the whole story is rushed to the composing room and is set while the headline is being written. If the headline is made up of several parts, it also is sent in takes, the first being slugged "C Hd Harbor Fog" and the second, if it is the last, "First and Last Ad C Hd Harbor Fog."

Under this system the type, as it is set, is taken to the proper page form and placed in the desired position. By deadline, all is placed except, possibly, the last "add" of the headline and that can be quickly set and rushed to the form. If, however, the copy desk had held the whole story until it had been edited and the headline written, the story would have missed the first edition.

In the foregoing case, the story was closed by the copy desk with the slug "Third and Last Ad Harbor Fog," but if there had been time to get more of the story into the first edition, the additional copy could have been sent with the slug "Ad All Harbor Fog," "Second Ad All Harbor Fog," etc. If there is only one take of additional matter, a simple method is to slug it "Ad at End Harbor Fog."

[1] Some newspapers use the letter system to designate headlines, others the numerical system. In the former case, the letters A, B or C designate a headline, the type of which is invariable. No further description is required. The same is true of headlines designated by numerals.

Peters Jackson Dale

Harbor Fog C 50

A clammy fog that marked the final week of one of the wettest mays on record was still a factor in flying and shipping yesterday. Ocean liners and freghters were delayed in the early morning hours but managed to creep to their piers as the thick haze rose and fell in patches during the day.

Meanwhile nearly 20 airplanes that had made emergency landings at Newark Airport, Camden and Allentown; Pennsylvania, took off from these fields in the morning hours. Service at la Guardia Field, which had been shut down tightly at 10:30 P.M. Friday, wasresumed early yesterday, and the problem of accommodating the "back-log" of flights from other seaborad airports was serious for a few hours.

At Newark 6 planes that had cruised from Washington to New York where they were to be shipped later to France, landed late Friday night. They had the airporrt to themselves, since it is now closed to passenger airliners regularly scheduled under an order of the Civil Aeronautics Authority.

Passenger airliners unable to reach blanketed La Guardia Field had to turn back to Camden's central airport, and a few went to Allentown. Thrity-five of these planes were reported landing during Friday night and before dawn yesterday, carrying between two hundred and three hundred passengers, most of whom re-sumed their journeys yesterday morning as the ceiling lifted and visibility lengthened. Three United States army transport planes also were forced down at Camden.

To keep the port free of congestion, many of the planes deposited their pas-sengers and took off immediately again.

In the waters of the harbor visibility was reduced several times during the day to virtually nothing, but there was an occ asional breeze from the sea that

EXAMPLE I. HOW A PAGE OF COPY LOOKS

Peters is the writer's name; Jackson and Dale are the reporters who supplied the facts. "Harbor Fog" is the slug placed on the copy by the night editor. "C" indicates the type of head placed on the copy by the night editor. "50" indicates the space required (here a half column) placed on the copy by the night editor.

record reporters' names on schedule and delete	~~Peters Jackson Dale~~
delete space mark (it is to inform desk only)	*Harbor Fog C 5a*
L or ¶, paragraph mark, use either	A clammy fog that marked the final week of one of the wettest
upper case	mays on record was still a factor in flying and shipping yest
insert letter	Ocean liners and freghters were delayed in the early morning
delete, close up	~~hours~~ but managed to creep to their piers as the thick haze r
period	and fell in patches during the day
spell out	Meanwhile nearly 20 airplanes that had made emergency landing
abbreviate	Newark Airport, Camden and Allentown, Pennsylvania, took off
upper case	these fields in the morning hours. Service at la Guardia Fiel
separate	which had been shut down tightly at 10:30 P.M. Friday, wasres
	early yesterday, and the problem of accommodating the "back-l
transpose	of flights from other seaborad airports was serious for a few
	hours.
spell out	At Newark 6 planes that had cruised from Washington to New Yo
	where they were to be shipped later to France, landed late Fr
delete letter	night. They had the airpoirt to themselves, since it is now
transpose	closed to passenger airliners regularly scheduled under an or
	of the Civil Aeronautics Authority.
delete, close up	Passenger airliners unable to reach ~~blanketed~~ La Guardia fiel
	to turn back to Camden's central airport, and a few went to A
transpose	town. Thrity-five of these planes were reported landing durin
	Friday night and before dawn yesterday, carrying between
contract to figures	two hundred and three hundred passengers, most of whom resume
	their journeys yesterday morning as the ceiling lifted and
upper case	visibility lengthened. Three United States army transport pl
	also were forced down at Camden.
follow on mark	To keep the port free of congestion, many of the planes

age number
ontinuation of
ollow on mark

substitute word
period, deletion
delete, close up

bring together

lower case

elete, close up

uide line used to
onnect broken parts
o aid the compositor
use this method to
elete, since it does
ot obliterate and para-
raph can be restored if
eeded)

end mark, use either

(2)

~~deposited~~ discharged their passengers and took off immediately ~~again.~~

In the ~~waters of the~~ harbor visibility was reduced several times during the day to virtually nothing, but there was an occ asional breeze from the sea that cleared the channels from time to time, permitting ships to move cautiously. In the upper Harbor the ferry services reported that at no time had the haze deepened sufficiently to cause suspension or even serious disruption.

~~In mid-afternoon the fog began to clear again and the sun appeared, but even though most of the city was free of fog, it clung tenaciously to the waters adjacent to Quarantine and Sandy Hook.~~

In addition to three incoming passenger liners, the Acadia, Cristobal and Samaria, eight small passenger vessels headed to sea during the day. It also was an unusually busy day for freighters, with about (20) ships of this class reaching Quarantine by sundown.

(///) #

EXAMPLE 2. HOW THE COPY LOOKS WHEN EDITED

~~Peters~~ Jackson ~~Dale~~

Harbor Fog C ~~SQ~~ HTK

A clammy fog that marked the final week of one of the wettest mays on record was still a factor in flying and shipping yesterday. Ocean liners and freighters were delayed in the early morning ~~hours~~ but managed to creep to their piers as the thick haze rose and fell in patches during the day.

Meanwhile nearly 20 airplanes that had made emergency landings at Newark Airport, Camden and Allentown, Pennsylvania took off from these fields in the morning hours. Service at la Guardia Field, which had been shut down tightly at 10:30 P.M. Friday, was resumed early yesterday, and the problem of accommodating the "back-log" of flights from other seaboard airports was serious for a few hours.

more

First-Ad Harbor Fog

At Newark 6 planes that had cruised from Washington to New York where they were to be shipped later to France, landed late Friday night. They had the airport to themselves, since it is now closed to passenger airliners regularly scheduled under an order of the Civil Aeronautics Authority.

more

Second Ad Harbor Fog

Passenger airliners unable to reach ~~blanketed~~ La Guardia Field
d to turn back to Camden's central airport, and a few went to Allentown.
rity-five of these planes were reported landing during Friday night and before
wn yesterday, carrying between two hundred and three hundred passengers, most
whom resumed their journeys yesterday morning as the ceiling lifted and vis-
ility lengthened. Three United States army transport planes also were forced
wn at Camden.

To keep the port free of congestion, many of the planes discharged ~~deposited~~
eir passengers and took off immediately ~~again.~~

(More)

Third and last Ad Harbor Fog

In the ~~waters of the~~ harbor visibility was reduced several times
ring the day to virtually nothing, but there was an occ asional breeze from
e sea that cleared the channels from time to time, permitting ships to move
utiously. In the upper Harbor the ferry services reported that at no time
d the haze deepened sufficiently to cause suspension or even serious disruption.

~~In mid-afternoon the fog began to clear again and the sun appeared,~~
~~t even though most of the city was free of fog, it clung tenaciously to the~~
~~ters adjacent to Quarantine and at Sandy Hook.~~

In addition to three incoming passenger liners, the Acadia, Cristobal
d Samaria, eight small passenger vessels headed to sea during the day. It also
s an unusually busy day for freighters, with about 20 ships of this class
aching Quarantine by sundown.

(###)

EXAMPLE 3. SENDING THE COPY IN "TAKES"

Examples 1 to 3 show how a page of original copy looks, how a story is edited with the proper symbols and how a story is sent to the composing room in "takes."

In some offices cable copy is rewritten before it is sent to the copy desk. In offices where such copy goes at once to the desk, it is the task of the copy editor to supply omitted words as well as to edit the copy to correct errors in construction, accuracy, consistency and grammar. Example 4 shows how cable copy looks when edited.

THE END MARK

The end mark is an important detail of copy editing. When a story is completed, the end mark must be placed at the end. If no mark appears, the composing room has no way of knowing whether there is more coming and time is lost finding out.

INSERTS

It frequently happens that after the story and headline have been sent to the composing room, new information is received. If these new facts are too important to be sent as adds, an insert must be made. This piece of copy is slugged "Insert A-Harbor Fog." If the insert must be sent in takes, the second section is slugged "First Ad Insert A-Harbor Fog," and the next, if it is the last, is slugged "Second and Last Ad Insert A-Harbor Fog." At the end of the last take of an insert, the custom is to indicate the end by "End Insert A" rather than indicating by the end mark. Other inserts are lettered "B," "C," "D," etc.

NEW LEADS

There are other technical complications that face the copy editor. After the story has been sent to the composing room

~~622 NORSQUARE 19192 WAGONER~~ LONDON, ~~CRIME ONE~~

THE SECOND UNINATIONS CONGRESS ON CRIME PREVENTION ENDED TODAY WITH RECOMMENDATION AGAINST USING TERM "JUVENILE DELIQUENCY" FOR THE PETTY MISCONDUCT AND "MALADJUSTED BEHAVIOR" OF MINARS.

IT ALOS ~~RE~~PRODUCED ~~UNANTICIPATED~~ AGREEMENT BETWEEN HEADS OF UNISTATES AND ~~SOVUNION~~ DELEGATIONS ON NEED FOR HOLDING SCHOOLS AS WELL AS FAMILY RESPONSIBLE FOR DEALING WITH PROBLEM OF JUVENILE OFFENDERS.

A RESOLUTION PASSED BY EIGHTYFOUR-NATION CONFERENCE ON ITS FINAL DAY CAUTIONED AGAINST BOTH EXAGGERATING EXTENT OF JUVENILE DELIQUENCY AND USING TERM TOO GLIBLY.

STATING THAT ~~PROBLEM~~ "CANNOT BE CONSIDERED INDEPENDENTLY OF THE SOCIAL STRUCTURE OF THE STATE," RESOLUTION CONTINUED:

"IT SHOULD BE NOTED THAT ITS RECORDED INCREASE IS PARTLY DUE TO THE FACT THAT TODAY A LARGE NUMBER OF CASES ARE RECOGNIZED BECAUSE OF A BETTER ORGANIZATION OF PREVENTION AND TREATMENT, AND MOREOVER TO THE FACT THAT CERTAIN COUNTRIES INCLUDE INDELINQUENCY A SERIES OF MINOR ACTS OF INDISCIPLINE OR SOCIAL MALADJUSTMENT."

~~X~~ MORE.

EXAMPLE 4. HOW CABLE COPY LOOKS WHEN EDITED

and is set in type, there may be new developments that are more important than those already told. This requires that a new lead be written. This copy is slugged "New Lead Harbor Fog-Sub C-H.T.K." The next section, if there is one, is slugged "First Ad New Lead Harbor Fog" and "more" is marked at the end. The next take, if it is the last, is slugged "Second and Last Ad New Lead Harbor Fog." The end of the last take is marked "End New Lead Turn Rule for Pickup."

MARKING THE PROOF

The new lead is now in the composing room. It remains for the copy editor to write the substitute head and to indicate where the inserts are to go and how much of the old story must be "killed" for the new lead. This is done on the galley proof. If the new lead has been properly written, it is necessary only to "kill" the old lead and mark the proof "Turn Rule for New Lead." The places where the inserts fit into the sequence of the story are marked "Turn Rule for Insert A," "Turn Rule for Insert B," etc. If the new lead does not fit properly without editing the old type, this also must be done in proof.

Turning the rule means to invert the rule, which is a strip of brass or type metal of the height of the type, so that the broad edge is up. This indicates that a correction or alteration is to be made at that point in the type. If the rule should be left turned, a broad black line would appear in the newspaper at that point. To the experienced printer, however, a turned rule can be seen at a glance in a page of type and is a warning sign.

The corrected proofs are then sent to the composing room, the corrected old type is reset and is sent with the marked proofs to the proper page form. The printer then puts in the new lead, replaces such of the old type as has been corrected, places the inserts as indicated and substitutes the new head for

85-G

SUN—TRAIN—

SERVICE MEN GET NEW PROTECTION

Law Now Safeguards Job Rights of Reservists and Guardsmen in Training

G. MAYS

Military reservists and National Guardsmen, both Army and Air, who leave their jobs for periods of training will be entitled to additional re-employment rights under Federal law, beginning Sept. 10.

These rights wil become effective under recently enacted amendments to the Universal Military Training and Service Act. The legislation, signed on July 12 by President Eisenhower, was sponsored by the Departments of Labor and Defense.

It protects reservists and guardsmen from loss of seniority, status and pay. It also provides that an employe need not accede to his employer's demand that he take his training during his normal vacation period if he does not wish to do so.

G. MAYS

Disability Provision

Among other protections under the new law, persons who become disabled while in training and cannot perform their regular jobs will be entitled to re-employment in other jobs that they can fill. If hospitalized while in training, they may delay application for re-employment up to one year.

James T. O'Connell, Under Secretary of Labor, emphasized yesterday that reservists and guardsmen must request a leave of absence from their employers before departing for military training.

He said that they must report for re-employment at the next regular scheduled working period after their return from training, or within a reasonabl- time thereafter if delay- cause of facto- control. F- point-

106-G

sun--cemetery

CEMETERY ASKING STATE HELP IN SUIT

Bids Attorney General Step Into Case Involving Fees for Outside Gardeners

CEMETERY h. chandler—

The State Board of Cemeteries last week asked the State Attorney General to intervene in a suit in Supreme Court to defend a schedule of cemetery fees that the board had approved.

The case involves Washington Cemetery at Bay Parkway and McDonald Avenue, Brooklyn.

Last year the cemetery reviewed its costs and decided it was incurring expenses when grave and plot owners engaged outside gardeners to care for family burial grounds. It instituted annual fees of $2 a grave and $10 a plot, to be paid by the gardeners for the privilege of entering the cemetery and working its grounds.

The gardening service provided by the cemetery is in competition with the outside gardeners.

The fees and the cost data on which they were based were reviewed last December by the State Board of Cemeteries. This board consists of Mrs. Caroline K. Simon, Secretary of State, chairman, and representative of the Attorney General and the State Health Commissioner. The board approved the cemetery's action.

A suit challenging the legality of the fees was brought by M. Goldsmith, Inc., florist and gardener, of 1300 McDonald Avenue, just outside the cemetery. Goldsmith for many years has had commissions from lot owners to care for graves in the cemetery.

The cemetery's situatio- been complicated b- loss resulti- Abo-

EXAMPLE 5. HOW THE PROOF LOOKS

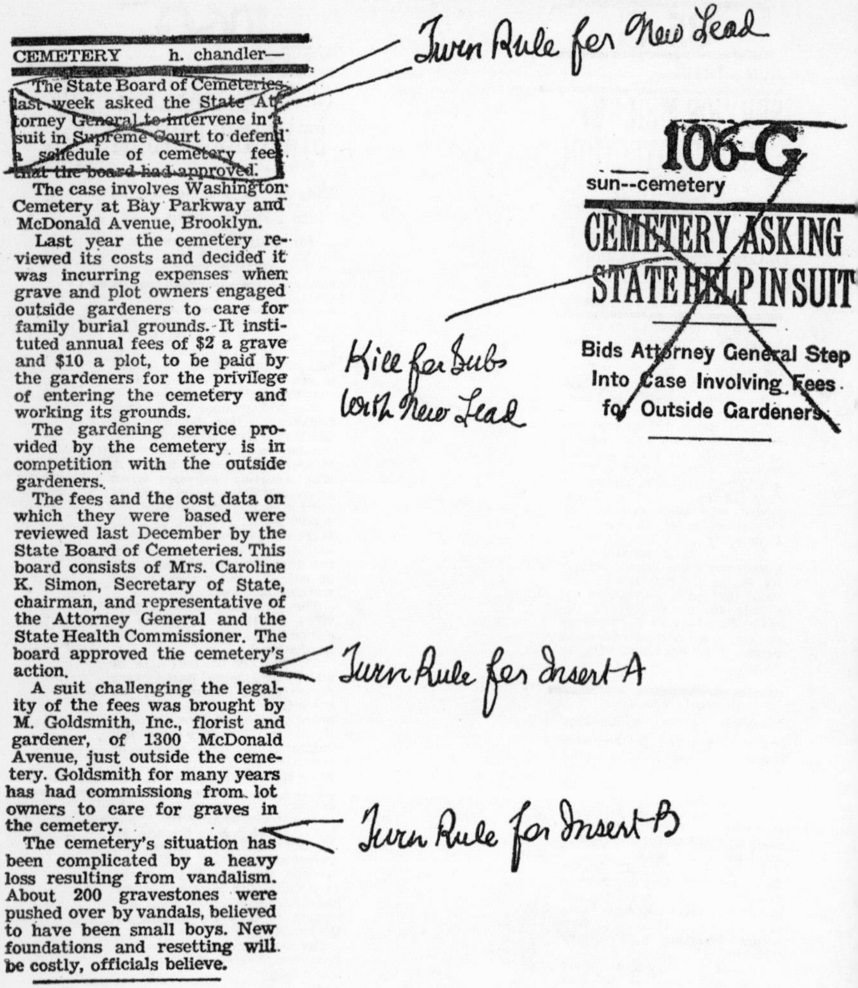

CEMETERY h. chandler—

The State Board of Cemeteries last week asked the State Attorney General to intervene in a suit in Supreme Court to defend a schedule of cemetery fees that the board had approved.

The case involves Washington Cemetery at Bay Parkway and McDonald Avenue, Brooklyn.

Last year the cemetery reviewed its costs and decided it was incurring expenses when grave and plot owners engaged outside gardeners to care for family burial grounds. It instituted annual fees of $2 a grave and $10 a plot, to be paid by the gardeners for the privilege of entering the cemetery and working its grounds.

The gardening service provided by the cemetery is in competition with the outside gardeners.

The fees and the cost data on which they were based were reviewed last December by the State Board of Cemeteries. This board consists of Mrs. Caroline K. Simon, Secretary of State, chairman, and representative of the Attorney General and the State Health Commissioner. The board approved the cemetery's action.

A suit challenging the legality of the fees was brought by M. Goldsmith, Inc., florist and gardener, of 1300 McDonald Avenue, just outside the cemetery. Goldsmith for many years has had commissions from lot owners to care for graves in the cemetery.

The cemetery's situation has been complicated by a heavy loss resulting from vandalism. About 200 gravestones were pushed over by vandals, believed to have been small boys. New foundations and resetting will be costly, officials believe.

106-G

sun--cemetery

CEMETERY ASKING STATE HELP IN SUIT

Bids Attorney General Step Into Case Involving Fees for Outside Gardeners

Turn Rule for New Lead

Kill for Subs With New Lead

Turn Rule for Insert A

Turn Rule for Insert B

EXAMPLE 6. HOW THE PROOF IS MARKED

the old. Examples 5 and 6 show how proof looks and how it is marked.

LEAD TO COME

When an event is to take place close to the newspaper's deadline, "lead to come" copy, sometimes called "B copy," often is written in advance so that an adequate report can be printed in the first edition. This is frequently done in the case of political meetings. Minor details, background material and a list of speakers can be given to elaborate the story for one edition. This is sent to the copy desk for editing long before the lead is written, and is slugged "Lead to Come-Governor," for example.

When the speeches at the meeting have been made, the reporter telephones his facts to a rewrite man who writes the lead. The desk slugs this copy "Lead Governor" and at the end of the lead marks "End Lead Pick Up Lead to Come Matter in Type."

ENDING PAGES ON PARAGRAPHS

News stories should be written so that a completed paragraph ends each page. This practice has fallen into disuse but is still important, because it saves time for the copy desk and the composing room. It is imperative that each page of "running stories," which must be sent in takes, end with a completed paragraph. If it does not, the copy editor must clip and paste, losing time when it is most necessary. If the reporter does not follow this rule, the copy editor must. It is obvious for mechanical reasons that a take of copy that stops with an unfinished sentence cannot be sent to the composing room. If the take ends with a period, the copy editor may send it on, but he must make a paragraph arbitrarily at the beginning of the next take.

NUMBERING PAGES

Every sheet of copy, except the first, must be numbered, the numbers running consecutively.

The dropping of a number results in inquiries from the composing room. In the case of a sectional story, the numbering of sheets does not run consecutively to the end of the story, but starts anew with each take.

JUMP HEADS

Most front page stories "jump" or continue to an inside page. The jumped type carries a "jump head" which on some newspapers duplicates the top lines of the front page head. This is required so that the continuation of the story may be identified easily. On others one or two key words are used to identify the continuation, such as "U.N. Debate," "Fatal Crash," "Slum Case" etc.

ESTIMATING SPACE

One system of estimating space is by the stick, which is about two inches of type, or about one-tenth of a column. The name stick comes from the days of hand typesetting, a stick being the small metal tray in which the printer placed the type as he set it. The amount of type that could be set in this tray was about two inches, hence the use of the term as a space measurement.

A simple method is one known as the unit system, 100 representing a column of type, 50 a half-column, 10 one-tenth of a column, etc. Thus 75 marked on copy by the editor in charge indicates that the space allowed for the story is three-fourths of a column. The copy editor should keep in mind that such space indication means that the story and the headline must not exceed that limit. The space required by the headline, therefore, must be taken into consideration in reducing the length of the story.

Space can be measured also by number of words. In this system 1,000 words is taken as the approximate number in a column of type, making 500 words a half-column, 100 one-tenth of a column, etc.

The size of the type and the width of the column are the basic factors in determining the number of words that fill a column. It is obvious that much more agate, or 5½ point, type than 10 point type will go into a column. Body types in general use by newspapers are 7 point, 8 point, 8½ point, and 9 point. The trend is toward larger body type. In changing from 7 point to 8 point the number of words to the column is reduced by some 50 to 100 words. Likewise more words can be printed in a column 12 ems wide than in a column 11 ems wide.

These are technical matters which the copy editor should know, and which the novice or the student of journalism will learn in time. But it is enough for practical desk work to know that 100 lines of typewritten copy, averaging ten words to the line, if set in standard type, will fit into a standard newspaper column, not including the head.

THE SCHEDULE

The copy editor's schedule is a record of his daily or nightly work. Not only is it the office's record of the writer and the editor of the copy, it is also the copy editor's guide. On it are noted every story he edits, every add, new lead, insert, the headline, substitute headlines, the writer of the story and his source of information, the length and the slug. By it the copy editor can determine every operation in connection with every story that has gone through his hands.

5. ABUSED WORDS

THE FOLLOWING list of words, commonly misused by newspaper reporters and copy editors, has been compiled with the objects of helping to promote a discriminating use of English and of overcoming some of the stereotyped expressions found most frequently. It is an attempt to show by example how news copy can be made more expressive and direct and how clichés that survive by tradition in each generation of newspaper men can be eliminated. It is hoped that such a list will be of value in the newspaper office as well as to the student of journalism. It is necessarily a limited list. For extended discussion the reader is referred to *Watch Your Language* by Theodore M. Bernstein (Channel Press, 1958).

It should be kept in mind that preferred uses have been indicated for each word only in conjunction with the word coupled with it and no attempt has been made to show proper uses in other senses.

This compilation is not designed to be exhaustive. It is not, and is not intended to be, a substitute for the dictionary; rather its use should stimulate attention to accurate definition and consequently bring about more discriminating use of words.

ACCORD—GRANT *Accord* is an important-sounding word for which *grant* usually is better. *He accorded many favors* is correct but *He granted many favors* is simpler and preferable in newspaper writing. *Accord* should be used sparingly except on ceremonious or extremely important occasions.

ACT—ACTION *The Governor's act in signing the bill was one step in the course of action he had outlined for public improvements.* An action may be composed of many acts.

ADMINISTER—DEAL *The blow was administered from behind* should read *The blow was dealt from behind.* However, *The Mayor administered the oath, The physician administered the medicine* and *The President administered the affairs of the nation with success* are correct.

ADOPT—DECIDE UPON—ASSUME *The Legislature adopted the resolution. He decided upon* (not adopted) *the course he had mapped out. He assumed* (not adopted) *the role of burglar.*

ADVENT—ARRIVAL *Advent* is a ceremonious word and should be reserved for such occasions. *Arrival* is simpler and adequate to most purposes. *The advent of the King's party was colorful and solemn. His arrival after dinner was expected.*

AFFECT *see* Effect

ALLEGE—SAY *Alleged* is an overworked newspaper word. *Alleged crime* is correct but *alleged criminal* is not, although the latter expression may be condoned because it is the briefest way to express the status of the incriminated person. Suspect or prisoner often will serve for *alleged criminal. He said* (not alleged) *he was innocent*, but *He alleged his innocence.* Also, *He said* (not alleged) *that he had flown to Greenland.*

ALL OF The *of* is unnecessary. *The robber took all of the money* should be *The robber took all the money.*

ALLUDE—REFER The editor can determine only from the text of a statement whether *allusion* or *reference* has been made. *He alluded to strife in the party when he said, "We have had troubles enough."* (Not mentioning directly.) *He referred to strife in the party when he said, "Let us end this internal dissension."* (Mentioning directly.)

ALONE—ONLY *The lawyer said that fright alone could have caused the man's death* means that fright, without the aid of anything else, could have caused the death. *The lawyer said that fright only could have caused the man's death* means that nothing else than fright could have done so.

ALTERNATIVE—COURSE *He had no course* (not alternative) *but to flee. These are the only courses* (not alternatives). *The alternative was to fight or to flee.*

AMATEUR—NOVICE *The amateur's skill exceeded the professional player's. The novice began his course of instruction at the age of ten.*

AMONG—BETWEEN *He distinguished between the two objects. He must share it among five persons.*

AND—TO *Try and do it* is popular, but nevertheless is a vulgarism. *Try to do it* is correct. *Come to* (not and) *see me. He planned to go to the capital to see the Senator* does not mean the same thing as *He planned to go to the capital and see the Senator.*

ANTICIPATE—EXPECT *He anticipated the result and was prepared to try another plan. He expected no other result.*

ANXIOUS—EAGER *He was anxious over the outcome of the election. He was eager* (not anxious) *to go.*

APPRECIATE—VALUE HIGHLY *He appreciated the significance of the overture* means that he put the proper construction upon it. *He valued highly* (not appreciated) *the praise of his colleagues.* It also is better to say *The land increased* (not appreciated) *in value.*

APPROVE *see* Indorse

ARRIVAL *see* Advent

AS, AS—SO, AS In affirmative comparisons *as, as* is correct, in negative *so, as. This is as good as that. This is not so good as that.*

AS IF *As if* is correct. *He looked as* (he would look) *though he were afraid* is absurd. *He looked as* (he would look) *if he were afraid* is correct.

ASSENT *see* Consent

ASSUME *see* Adopt

AUDIENCE—SPECTATORS An *audience* hears; *spectators* see.

AUTHENTIC *see* Genuine

AVENGE A person may *avenge* an injury done to him and take *revenge* for an injury done to others than himself.

AVOID—AVERT *The accident was averted when the captain avoided the reef.*

BALANCE—REMAINDER *Balance* often is used indiscriminately for *remainder. His balance at the bank was five dollars. The remainder* (not balance) *of the day was wasted;* or better still, *The rest of the day was wasted.*

BEGIN, END—COMMENCE, COMPLETE In almost all cases *begin* is preferable to *commence* in newspaper work. *Begin* and *end* are antonyms, as are *commence* and *complete.* A work of art is commenced and completed only when it has been perfected. A project may be begun and ended without being completed. *See also* Inaugurate.

BESIDE—BESIDES *Beside* is always a preposition. *Besides* is both a preposition and an adverb. *He stood beside the table; Besides the book, he has the manuscript; Besides, he will not go.*

BETWEEN *see* Among

BLAME IT ON This is a colloquial expression. The verb form is *blame*, not blame on. *The accident happened at noon; it was blamed on the engineer.* How much better to say, *The accident happened at noon; the engineer was blamed.* It is better also to write *He said the tide caused the collision* than *He blamed the tide*, because only persons can be considered blameworthy.

BRAVERY—COURAGE A policeman in a fight with robbers demonstrates his *bravery*. A timid man, having considered the dangers, shows *courage* in becoming a policeman.

BUT *see* Else

BY—OF—WITH—FOR *A man by the name of Smith* should read *A man of the name of Smith. He was afflicted with* (not by) *rheumatism. He was distinguished for* (not by) *his learning.* However, *In comparison with that landscape, this picture is distinguished by its colors.*

CANINE—DOG *Canine* does not mean a *dog*. *Canine* is the adjective, *dog* the noun.

CLAIM—SAY *He claimed the property* is correct. *He claimed that he had been there* is improved by writing *He said that he had been there* or, if it is a matter of dispute, *He contended that he had been there. Claim a right* is correct but *assert a right* probably is preferable.

CLIMAX This word is a noun and its use as a verb is not only improper but unnecessary. *A day of important events was climaxed by the President's address* should be changed to *The President's address was the climax of a day of important events.*

COMMENCE *see* Begin

COMMONLY *see* Generally

COMPARE WITH—COMPARE TO *Lee's strategy in his campaigns can be compared to Napoleon's. He was compared with their former leader and found wanting in daring.*

COMPLETE *see* Begin

CONCLUDE—END Speeches, meetings and hearings are *closed* or *ended*, not *concluded. He concluded his argument and then went on to explain its implications.*

CONDEMN *see* Criticize

CONSENT—ASSENT *He consented to go to the conference but refused to assent to the interpretation of the treaty that representation must be limited.*

CONSERVATIVE—MODERATE *He was a conservative in politics. He made a moderate* (not conservative) *estimate.*

CONSIDER—THINK *After long study, he said he considered the course unwise. He thinks the course is unwise. Think* does not necessarily exclude deliberation, but ordinarily is used in a more casual sense than consider.

CONTINUOUS—CONTINUAL A succession of showers is *continual;* a steady downpour is *continuous.*

COURAGE *see* Bravery

COURSE *see* Alternative

CRITICALLY—SERIOUSLY *Critically* is frequently used when seriously or gravely express the intent better. *Critically ill* specifies a certain stage of the disease.

CRITICIZE—CONDEMN *He criticized the book favorably. He condemned the book on the ground that it was propaganda.*

CUSTOMER *see* Patron

DEAL *see* Administer

DECIDE UPON *see* Adopt

DIE OF *One dies of disease* (not dies with, nor dies from, disease). However, *one suffers from disease* (not with it) and is *afflicted with blindness* (not by it).

DIMENSIONS *see* Proportions

DISTRICT *see* Section

DOG *see* Canine

EAGER *see* Anxious

EARN *see* Make

EFFECT—AFFECT *The policeman effected the rescue at great risk to himself but he was not affected by his strenuous efforts.* The word *effect* is considerably overused in newspapers, however. *He effected the capture of the robbers quickly* would be improved by *He captured the robbers quickly.*

ELSE—BUT *Nothing else than* (not but) *repudiation will be accepted.*

END *see* Begin; Conclude

ENTAIL *see* Involve

ESSENTIAL—NECESSARY *Freedom is essential to Democracy. Food is necessary to life.*

EVIDENCE—TESTIMONY *The evidence established the fact that he was the slayer. Testimony,* the statement of witnesses, may or may not be evidence.

EX—FORMER *Ex* is the Latin prefix meaning out or out of. It is often used to mean former, as ex-president. *Former* is to be preferred where brevity is not essential, as it is in the newspaper headline.

EXPECT *see* Anticipate

EXTEND—OFFER—SHOW *He extended his arm. He offered* (or sent, not extended) *the invitation. He showed* (not extended) *the courtesies required by the occasion.*

FAIL *He failed to pick it up* means that he tried but did not succeed. *The automobile failed to hit the man* is not possible.

FARTHER—FURTHER *The museum is farther away than the library. We will discuss it further.*

FEWER *see* Less

FIX *He fixed the ornament to the wall* and *He fixed the boundaries* are correct. Such expressions as *I'll fix him, He fixed the motor* and *He is well fixed* are colloquial.

FORMER *see* Ex

FORWARD Not *forwards.* It is preferable not to use the final s on words like *homeward, backward, toward.*

FREAK—FREAKISH *Freak* is the noun, *freakish* the adjective. *Freakish* (not freak) *storm.*

FREQUENTLY *see* Generally

FURTHER *see* Farther

GENERALLY—COMMONLY—FREQUENTLY—USUALLY These words are defined by Crabb thus: "*What is commonly done is an action common to all; what is generally done is the action of the greatest part; what is frequently done is either the action of the many, or an action many times repeated by the same person; what is usually done is done regularly by one or by many. Commonly is opposed to rarely; generally and frequently to occasionally or seldom; usually to casually.*"

GENUINE—AUTHENTIC *The manuscript was traced to Shakespeare, thus proving it genuine. The book is authentic as far as it relates to the economic history of the country, but is inaccurate in dealing with the cultural development.*

GET *see* Secure

GIANT—GIGANTIC *Giant* is both noun and adjective; *gigantic* always an adjective. *The gigantic* (not giant) *dirigible* is preferable.

GOTTEN—GOT It cannot be said that *gotten* is incorrect; it is merely falling into disuse in this country. *Got* is preferred, although the Anglo-Saxon verb is often so harsh that the softer Latin *obtained* is better. In such sentences as *I have got the book, got* is superflous.

GRANT *see* Accord

GUN—PISTOL A *gun*, generally speaking, is a large weapon. *Pistol* is the general name of small firearms, of which the revolver and the automatic pistol are the common types.

HANGED—HUNG Men are *hanged;* things are *hung.*

HAPPEN—OCCUR—TAKE PLACE *The accident happened* (or occurred) *suddenly. The party took place as scheduled. See also* Transpire

HEALTHY—HEALTHFUL—WHOLESOME *The animal was healthy. The climate was healthful. The food was wholesome.*

HUNG *see* Hanged

ILLY—ILL *Ill* is both adjective and adverb, and is preferable to *illy.*

IMPLICATE *see* Involve

INAUGURATE—BEGIN *The President was inaugurated. The project was begun* (not inaugurated).

INCUR *see* Sustain

INDIVIDUAL *see* Person

INDORSE—APPROVE These words have become indistinguishable in newspaper writing but *approve* is ordinarily the proper word. *He indorsed the check. He approved* (not indorsed) *the candidate.*

INVOLVE—IMPLICATE—ENTAIL *He was involved in a long series of disputes. He was implicated in the crime. The project entailed* (not involved) *the levying of new taxes.*

JUNCTURE—TIME *At this juncture,* as meaning a critical time, is somewhat stilted. *At this point* or *at this time* are better.

KIND OF A The article *a* after *kind of* is incorrect. *That kind of house.*

LADY—WOMAN *Woman* is always used in newspaper writing unless *lady* is a title properly applied to an Englishwoman. *Female* for *woman* is a vulgarism.

LAST—LATTER *Latter* is used in speaking of two things only; *last* is used in connection with more than two things.

LEND *see* Loan

LENGTHY—LONG *Long* is preferred. *Lengthy* seems to be used repeatedly to denote a greater duration than *long* but it does not.

LESS—FEWER *He bought less than a pound. There were fewer than twenty persons.*

LIMITED—SMALL *A man of small* (not limited) *means. The slight* (not limited) *application of the law. The range of the gun was short* (not limited).

LIVE *see* Reside

LOAN—LEND *Loan* is the noun; *lend* is the proper verb. *He lent* (not loaned) *the book. A million dollars was loaned* is commonly used and is correct, but even in the financial sense *lend* is better.

LOCATE—SETTLE—SITUATE *They settled* (not located) *on the river bank. The new city hall was located* (that is, its place determined) *on the hill. The city was situated* (not located) *between two rivers. The man was found* (not located) *at home.*

LONG *see* Lengthy

MAJORITY *see* Plurality

MAKE—EARN *He makes shoes for a living. He earns* (not makes) *ten dollars an hour.*

MARRY—IS MARRIED It is commonly accepted as proper to say that a man *marries* a woman and that a woman *is married to* a man.

MODERATE *see* Conservative

MUTUAL *A mutual friendship existed between the two. A common friendship existed among the three. They met at the house of a common* (not mutual) *friend.*

NECESSARY *see* Essential

NICE *This requires a nice distinction* is correct but *A nice day* is colloquial.

NOVEL *see* Unique.

NOVICE *see* Amateur

OCCUR *see* Happen; Transpire

ODD *see* Peculiar

OFFER *see* Extend

OFF OF *He fell off* (not off of) *the horse.*

ONLY *see* Alone

OUGHT—SHOULD *One ought to be honest. One should go to town today.*

PART *see* Portion

PARTIALLY—PARTLY *It is partly* (not partially) *done. It was done in a partial spirit.*

PARTY *see* Person

PATRON—CUSTOMER *The wealthy are patrons of the arts.* The

phrase *patron of the theater* commonly means only a spectator or a member of the audience.

PAY *see* Settle

PECULIAR—ODD *Speech was his peculiar gift. It was an odd circumstance.*

PEOPLE *see* Person

PER—A *Per* is often used in such phrases as *per day* and *per year.* It is better not to mix Latin and English. *A day, a year* should be used, or *per diem, per annum.*

PERSON—PEOPLE—PARTY—INDIVIDUAL *Forty persons* (not people) *were injured. This people is peace-loving. This person* (not party) *is being sued. This party to the suit is a banker. This party* (group of persons) *is composed of bankers. Neither this group of persons nor this individual* (of the group) *should be sued. A strange person* (not individual) *arrived.*

PISTOL *see* Gun

PLURALITY—MAJORITY *He won the election by a plurality of 140 votes and a majority of 110 votes. He received 200, his nearest opponent 60 and the only other candidate 30.*

POISONOUS—POISONED—VENOMOUS *The weed is poisonous. The snake is venomous. Poisoned* is a participial adjective and carries the active sense of the verb. One should discriminate between *poisoned food* and *poisonous food. Poison liquor,* an expression once seen in newspaper headlines, employs a noun as an adjective and has no grammatical justification.

PORTION—PART *In the division of the estate, his portion was small. That part of the machine is rusty.*

PRACTICALLY—VIRTUALLY *Practically* and *virtually* are used synonymously in newspaper writing to mean *almost.* In common usage this is not incorrect but a distinction would lead to a more agreeable variation. *This timber can be used practically as a foundation for the building* is a discriminating use of the word. *This seems to be virtually impossible but it can be done. The building is almost* (not practically) *completed.*

PREJUDICE—PREPOSSESS *He was prejudiced against the plan. He was prepossessed in favor of the plan.*

PROPORTIONS—DIMENSIONS *The proportions of the building were pleasing. A rock of huge dimensions* (not proportions). *The close division on the amendment was held to presage opposition of some proportions* (strength) *when the resolution reaches the floor.*

PROPOSE—PURPOSE *He proposed that the city build the bridge. He purposed fighting for his plan to the end.*

PUPIL *see* Scholar

PURPOSE *see* Propose

RAISE—REAR Animals are raised, children and buildings reared.

RECEIVE *see* Sustain

REFER *see* Allude

REMAINDER *see* Balance

RESIDE—LIVE *Live* is always better than *reside.* So also is home or house for residence.

REVENGE *see* Avenge

SAY *see* Allege; Claim; State

SCHOLAR—PUPIL—STUDENT *He is a scholar of world renown. This pupil has been under instruction for five years but is not yet ready for independent study. The students in the universities have shown seriousness of purpose. As a student of life he has learned much not taught in colleges.*

SECTION—DISTRICT *Section* is used indiscriminately for region, district, neighborhood or vicinity. *This neighborhood* (or vicinity) *is composed entirely of shops. The legislation seeks the unity of the port district. This section of the country was a stronghold of the Prohibition forces. He surveyed the north-polar region.*

SECURE—GET *The liner was secured to the dock. He got* (not secured) *the job.*

SERIOUSLY *see* Critically

SETTLE—PAY *They settled their dispute. He paid the bill. See also* Locate

SHOULD *see* Ought

SHOW *see* Extend

SITUATE *see* Locate

SMALL *see* Limited

SO *see* Such

SO, AS *see* As, As—So, As

SPECTATORS *see* Audience

STANDPOINT—VIEWPOINT *Viewpoint* or *point of view* usually is better.

STATE—SAY *He stated the position of the government in a two-hour address. He said* (not stated) *that he would go.*

STOP—STAY *He stayed* (not stopped) *at the hotel.*

STUDENT *see* Scholar

SUCH—SO *It was such a grave error that its effects can not be predicted* is incorrect. It should read *It was so grave an error that its effects can not be predicted.*

SUSTAIN—RECEIVE—INCUR *Bread sustains life. He received* (not sustained) *injuries. He incurred* (not sustained) *losses.*

TAKE PLACE *see* Happen

TESTIMONY *see* Evidence

THINK *see* Consider

TIME *see* Juncture

TO *see* And—To

TRANSPIRE—OCCUR *It transpired long afterward that the incident had occurred at the secret meeting in Geneva.*

UNIQUE—NOVEL *The art of Benvenuto Cellini is unique. The hostess devised a novel way of entertaining her guests. Most unique* is never correct.

USUALLY *see* Generally

VALUE HIGHLY *see* Appreciate

VENOMOUS *see* Poisonous

VIEWPOINT *see* Standpoint

VIRTUALLY *see* Practically

WHENCE *He returned whence* (not from whence) *he came.*

WHOLESOME *see* Healthy

WOMAN *see* Lady

PART TWO. THE HEADLINE

6. WHAT THE HEADLINE IS

A HEADLINE WRITER who boasted that he was engaged in producing a literary art form promptly would be set down as an intellectual climber. Yet such a boast would not be without basis. For the headline is a form of expression having fully as many standards to be met and requirements to be filled as, say, the sonnet or the triolet, with the important additional one of visual form. The difference, of course, lies in the end-all—in one case it is beauty, in the other utility.

The headline's function is much like that of a commercial sample—the small tube of tooth paste distributed free at the dentists' convention, the guest-size bar of soap that you find in your hotel room. The headline is like the trial tube of tooth paste and, parenthetically, if it is set in sufficiently large type it is really free. The tiny tube aims at giving the prospective consumer accurate and complete information about the product, at giving the information in a quick and easy form and at presenting it so attractively that he will be impelled to form an attachment for the product. The headline's aim is the same: to present accurate and complete information quickly and attractively. The product to be sold is the news story.

Modern newspapers are designed to inform, and to inform as rapidly as possible. This purpose led to the development of the news lead—the opening of a story which packs into a paragraph or two all the essential information contained in the article. The headline carries the condensation process a step further. Where the lead speaks in terms of sentences and paragraphs, the headline speaks in terms of words. The headline is, in a sense, a super lead, and to facilitate rapid reading, display type is used. The large letters also serve to dress up the page typographically, but primarily they are employed to help the reader get at a glance what he wants to know.

As many readers keep posted on daily happenings almost entirely by scanning the headlines, the copy editor must incorporate as much information as possible in the head, must present it with unswerving accuracy and must emphasize the important point or points of the news. The technique of doing this will be taken up later. The present purpose is to discover what the headline is and how it developed.

Captions are probably as old as writing, but captions are not headlines. Titles for articles serve, for one thing, to mark off clearly where the articles begin. Often they apparently have no other purpose. Again in some cases they strive to give the reader an inkling of the information contained in the articles, but generally they accomplish this merely by labeling. In other cases titles are deliberately mysterious, alluring, seeking to tempt the reader into perusing what follows. Rarely are they both informative and alluring, as the modern headline frequently is.

In journalism of the English language we come across efforts to digest information and to present it in readily readable form as early as 1625. In that year a newspaper issued in London by a group of men, most prominent among whom was Nathaniel Butter, appeared with the following front page:

The
CONTINUATION
of our weekly
Newes, from the 24 of February
to the 2 of March

Wherein is contained the present state of Count
Mansfield's Armse. The preparation of the
Prince of Orange with the continuation of the siege
of Breda.
The late surprisall of the Towne of Soeft by the Colonell
Gent.
The warre-like preparations of Bethlem Gabor being aided
by the Grand Signior
with the invasion of the Count of Thurne in Germany.
As also the proceedings which were lately made by the
French forces in Veltoline.
Besides the great contributions which have beene given
to the King of Spaine to maintain the warres. With
divers other particulars.
From Rome, Venice, Naples, Millan, Savoy
Germany, France, Denmark, the Low-Coun-
tries and divers other places of Christendome.

Aside from the obvious objection that these items do not head articles, they could in no sense be termed headlines. They do not divulge information, they tell *about* it. These are not the trial tubes of tooth paste mentioned before. They are merely the advertisements telling about the tooth paste. Wherein lies the distinction between the caption, or the label, and the modern headline? The chief point is the presence or absence of a verb. The distinction is between saying something and characterizing. The headline makes a statement, the caption calls names.

HOW HEADLINES DEVELOPED

Headlines are almost exclusively an American development. Newspapers in other parts of the world were until relatively recently content with captions. Therefore any sketch of the history of the headline concerns itself with American journalism.

The development of the headline in this country might

roughly be compared to the development of the speech of an infant. The baby's first words, if psychologists and parents are to be believed, are simple nouns: "mamma," "papa," "spoon," "table." Quickly the young linguist begins to add adjectives to its vocabulary and says: "nice papa," "pretty spoon," "big table." In newspaper headlines the earliest stage is similar; the captions speak in terms of nouns and adjectives: "Foreign Affairs," "Tragic Accident," "Charge of False Pretenses." At this stage neither the baby nor the headline can be considered as really saying anything. We can discern in a general way what both are driving at. When the baby says, "pretty spoon," we gather that it is pleased; when the newspaper says "Tragic Accident," we gather it is shocked. But no direct statement is being made.

Finally, however, both become articulate, and the deciding factor is the addition of the verb. The baby now says, "Gimme pretty spoon," "Nice papa come home," and the headline with its newly loosened tongue exclaims, "The Maine Blown Up" or "Two Held on Fraud Charge." Both have now come into their own, and the only difficulty is keeping the baby from talking too much and the headline from shouting too loudly.

Just when the headline began to assume its modern form cannot be told with any exactness, any more than it is possible to determine the moment when baby uttered its first verb. Just as the infant mumbles and squeals vague sounds that might be interpreted as verb forms before it actually speaks these forms clearly, so the headline made tentative, in some cases almost accidental, use of the verb before this came to be the recognized *sine qua non.*

From earliest times right up to the Spanish-American War days, the accepted headline form was the label. And this label was not infrequently a staple, the same one being used repeatedly. Aside from the usual departmental headings like "Foreign Affairs" or "Diurnal Occurences," there were the "stock" heads used on the leading news stories. An examination of the files of *The New-York Times* for 1860, for example, shows that the heading "The Presidential Campaign" was used time and time again, and during the Civil War the latest tidings from the front were recorded first under the caption "The National Crisis" and later under either "The Great Rebellion" or "The Rebellion Record." It would not be fair to assume that the reader got no information from the heading, for these captions were always followed by subordinate divisions—often nearly a dozen of them—and it was in these parts of the headline that the verb occasionally cropped up, sometimes, it seems, almost against the will of the caption writer. On November 7, 1860, in the heading recounting the results of the presidential election, we find one bank that reads: "The North Rises in Indignation at the Menaces of the South"; and another declaring, "Abraham Lincoln Probably Elected President by a Majority of the Entire Popular Vote." The eight other parts of the head, however, are barren of verbs.

One of the earliest captions having the ring of a modern headline appeared in an "extra" of *The Boston Gazette* on October 26, 1781. The extra was nothing more than a single-page leaflet issued to bulletin a great event in the history of the colonies. In large type at the top were the words: "Cornwallis Taken!" The journalistic genius of the editor, Edes, in getting out an extra in the first place was confirmed by his choice of a caption, which, even according to modern standards, could not be improved upon. Even this, however, must be set down as a flash of genius and nothing more, for such captions were not the rule in those days. Again on June 11, 1865, *The New-York Times* carried a frontpage heading:

"Steamer Sunk at Sea," which also smacks of the modern technique, but this, too, must be classed as a mere sport in the journalistic garden.

As indicated before, no line of demarcation is evident between the days of the caption and the days of the headline, but in a general way the war of 1898, during which the competition among newspapers to present the latest events speedily and luridly was intense, may be considered as the period that ushered in the headline that said something.

It was during this period, likewise, and in the years immediately preceding it that the headline was molded into its modern physical pattern. Before the Civil War, when the heading was nothing more than a caption, it was printed accordingly. Then in the intense days leading up to the war between the states, when the press underwent a rise in blood pressure and felt compelled to become a little more informative in its captions, large type and longer headings were used—sometimes they extended halfway down the page. But the type was a jumble of fonts, it still was comparatively small and it gave anything but a pleasing appearance, judged from today's point of view. The front page now contained three or four of these large heads, however, compared with the one or two it displayed in earlier days. By the time the Spanish-American War came along, the front page had assumed something of its present-day symmetry and the headlines had been dressed in more modern clothes, with tops of large display type and banks and crosslines that were in harmony.

Until this time, it must be remembered, the headline was kept closely imprisoned between the rules of a single column. *The Times,* it is true, had momentarily sawed through the bars on July 22, 1871, when it spread the headline (and story) of its Tweed Ring exposure across three columns, but this was exceptional. By the time of the blowing up of the battleship *Maine*, however, the papers had become more liberal jailkeepers and *The World* and *The Journal* in New York allowed the headlines on this stunning event to roam the full width of the page, thus introducing the familiar banner head of today. In addition, tremendous type was used, larger even than we have become accustomed to in present times. It remained for World War I to give the multi-column head a standing in polite journalistic society.

THE PRESENT TENSE

We have seen that the modern headline is distinguished by the fact that it says something—it makes a complete statement instead of merely characterizing. But in addition it speaks a language of its own. This language is not "headlinese," a perverted speech, of which more will be said later, but is merely pure English adapted to the requirements of headlining.

For one thing, the present tense is customarily used to describe past events. This usage is not something created by headline writers, but is simply something borrowed from everyday speech. The present tense is employed because it is the tense of immediacy, because it is more vivid and hence because it makes our trial tube of tooth paste more inviting to the prospective buyer.

The corner grocery store has just been held up. In a frenzy the proprietor dashes to the street and shouts for a policeman. Presently Patrolman Murphy comes jogging to the scene.

"What's the trouble, Mr. Brown?" he asks.

"I've been held up," says Mr. Brown. "Two hundred bucks . . . my watch . . . he took everything. A fine police force. Well, why don't you do something? Don't stand . . ."

"Wait a minute, wait a minute. I gotta know what happened. Tell me about it."

"Listen, Murphy. This bird comes into my store. He asks for a box of animal crackers. As soon as I turn to get it, he pulls a gun and sticks it into my back. He tells me to open the cash register. Then he cleans out the drawer, lifts my watch and beats it away faster than you could say Jack Robinson."

"O.K., Mr. Brown, I'll report it to headquarters."

This is a fair account of an everyday occurrence. Note how Mr. Brown describes the hold-up. No past tense for him. He is living the scene over again. And incidentally he is making Patrolman Murphy live it with him. That, in a sense, is what the present tense in the headline does. It puts the reader on the scene, it makes him a participant in the action, it brings the events into immediacy.

That is the prime reason for using the present tense, but there is another. In most instances verbs in the present tense are shorter than those in the past, and space is always in demand in the headline. It takes fewer letters, for example, to say "Thief Robs Grocery" than to say "Thief Robbed Grocery."

OMISSION OF MINOR WORDS

So the use of the present tense to describe past action is one characteristic of our headline language. Another characteristic, which is more obvious to the ordinary reader, is the omission of non-essential words, chiefly articles. This practice has a tendency to give the headline telegraphic speed, and hence to make it more vivid. But contrary to a prevalent impression among headline writers themselves, the effect of speed is not the object of omitting words; it is rather a happy by-product.

Words are left out in headlines simply for the sake of economy, just as they are in telegrams. To pretend there is any other reason is as idle in one instance as in the other.

Still another characteristic of headline language is the use of short words, mainly of Anglo-Saxon derivation. And here again the space requirement is the commanding factor.

Obviously, then, limitations of space impose a distinct handicap on the headline writer. He is expected to put on an intricate juggling act in a five-foot square cubicle. The wonder is that he can do it at all, much less do it well. In the next chapter we shall see why the space is so restricted, and then we shall set about discovering how the copy editor performs his feat.

7. HOW THE HEADLINE LOOKS

HEADLINES are bounded on the east and west by column rules. In the vertical direction their form is definitely fixed by patterns—patterns that vary for different newspapers and for different kinds of heads used by any one newspaper, but that remain the same for any one type of head on any one newspaper. These two restrictions are what set the bounds of the cubicle within which the copy editor stages his juggling tricks.

TYPOGRAPHICAL PATTERNS

While headline patterns show diversity throughout the United States, they have at least one feature in common. The topmost part of the head is set, almost without exception, in display type, while the succeeding parts alternate between small and large type or between small, light type and large, heavy type. Put in another way, alternate parts of the head, beginning with the topmost section, are chosen for emphasis, typographically at least.

All the forms in which the parts of a headline are set may be reduced to five basic classifications: drop or stepped lines, inverted pyramids, crosslines, hanging indentation, and flush-left. In addition, some papers employ two or more lines set flush to both margins, but this might almost be considered a variation of the drop line.

In the drop or stepped line form, the lines are of the same

length, but are symmetrically staggered like a flight of steps. If there are two lines, the first is set flush to the left-hand margin and the second to the right-hand margin; if there are three lines, the first is flush to the left-hand margin, the second indented from both margins and the third flush to the right-hand margin. Sometimes the flight has four and even five steps.

The inverted pyramid may include any number of lines, within reason, from two up. In this form, the lines following the top line taper; each line is shorter than the preceding one.

Crosslines are simply single lines of type. They may be set either to extend across the full width of the column or "centered."

The hanging indentation form, like the inverted pyramid, may include any number of lines within reason. The first line is the longest and the succeeding lines are indented at the left, each by the same amount, but are flush with the first line at the right. In this form the succeeding lines are said to hang from the first. While it is not necessary that the final line extend all the way to the right-hand margin, the typographical appearance is better if it does.

In the flush-left form the lines of the topmost part of the head are aligned close to the left-hand margin and are allowed to run ragged at the right. This form was devised to make the writing of the headline easier, less confined by typographical restrictions. For the succeeding subordinate part of this kind of headline various patterns have been tried. Some of them are not typographically successful; they have a tendency to drift uncomfortably in space. The banks seem to require either anchoring to one of the margins or stabilization by rules above and below them.

The following illustration will help in visualizing the first four of the five forms previously described.

DROP LINE FORM
LOOKS LIKE THIS

While These Lines Illustrate
the Appearance of an
Inverted Pyramid

AND THIS IS A CROSSLINE

Hanging Indentation Is Set
Like This and It Is Best If
Last Line Goes to Here

Incidentally, the illustration, if taken as representative of a headline, also shows the most common uses to which the typographical forms are put, that is, how they are employed in the various parts of a headline. It is not at all unusual, however, for drop lines to be used where the crossline now is, nor for the crossline to be employed as the topmost part. The illustrations on page 115 show four typical headlines, including all five typographical forms that have been described.

Two other typographical designs should be mentioned. One is simply a single line of type that may extend over many columns. This is called a ribbon and is used by newspapers that stress horizontal make-up. It is especially serviceable when a story has to be spread over a wide, shallow space on the page.

The other additional typographical design includes a subordinate line above a normal headline. This line, usually set flush to the left-hand margin and sometimes underlined, is called a kicker or a snapper or an eyebrow. It is sometimes used as a departmental designation such as "Theatre News" or

"Book Review." Other times it is used to include a subsidiary fact in the head, as in the example.

120 Planes to Fly From U. S.

Air Force Sets 'Exercise'
In the Far East Next Week

TERMINOLOGY OF THE PARTS

We have been referring to the "topmost part" of the headline and the "succeeding parts." Let us now give these various sections names so that we may refer to them more conveniently. In some newspaper offices every part of a headline is

State Board
Votes to Keep
Savings Rate

Retains Ceiling on
Interest Dividends

Executive, 60,
Leaving Post
For Ministry

Did His Studying On
Commuter Trains

Tour Experts
See Potential

Travel Writers Visit
City and Offer Ideas
for Development

WIN HONORARY DEGREE

TWO MINISTERS SELECTED
BY COLLEGES.

The Rev. Romans Smith and
the Rev. Ralph Roland
Are Recipients.

TYPICAL HEADLINE PATTERNS

New York Herald Tribune *New York World-Telegram and Sun*
Milwaukee Journal *Kansas City Star*

called a "deck." Other offices have a more precise system which we shall adopt. In these offices the word deck and its synonym "bank" are restricted to the subordinate parts of the headline having two or more lines. The topmost part of the head—the part that is set in large display type—is termed, logically enough, the "top." The parts of the head between the decks or banks, the parts set in more emphatic type than the decks, are usually styled "crosslines," even though they may not be crosslines in the typographical sense, but may be set as drop lines. This terminology, in addition to its advantage of being slightly more specific, conveys a better sense of what the parts referred to look like. Henceforth, then, we shall speak of the top, the first bank or deck, the crossline and the second or last bank or deck.

The top of the headline is, as has been noted, usually set in display type; it is the part that catches the eye first. It traditionally was set entirely in capital letters, although nowadays many papers use bold upper- and lower-case letters. Banks are customarily set in upper- and lower-case letters, while the crossline may be either in capitals or in capitals and small letters.

Virtually every newspaper office has a headline schedule, a chart showing samples of all the headlines used by that paper. The various heads are designated by letter or by number or, in some cases, by combinations of both. The largest single-column head, for example, might be styled an A head or a Number 1 head, the next largest a B head or a Number 2 head and so on. A number is often used to indicate the width of the head: A 3B head, for instance, would be a B head set three columns wide.

On some newspapers it is necessary for the copy editor in writing the headline to specify for the benefit of the composing room the styles and sizes of the type that the headline schedule provides, but on other papers the composing room is expected to know this and the copy editor merely marks the headline "A" or "B." In any case, the pattern of any one headline is unvarying. The top of the A head is not on one occasion set in thirty-six point type and on another in twenty-four point, nor does it on one occasion have two lines and on another three.

THE UNIT-COUNT SYSTEM

In any given size and style of type, the number of letters and of spaces between words that a line will accommodate is rigidly limited. For each headline the size and style of type are a given factor and it is the task of the copy editor, therefore, to make the lines fit the space. To accomplish this, he is equipped with a magic key—a key that will serve him on any newspaper for which he happens to be working. This key is simply a system of counting out the lines by units.

Printed letters are not all exactly the same width, although with certain exceptions they are approximately so. The following lines, each of which contains ten letters, show at a glance the relative widths of some of the letters:

AAAAAAAAAA
BBBBBBBBBB
CCCCCCCCCC
MMMMMMMMMM
WWWWWWWWWW
IIIIIIIIII
JJJJJJJJJJ
mmmmmmmmmm
wwwwwwwwww
iiiiiiiiii
llllllllll
ffffffffff

Obviously M and W are wider than other capital letters, just as m and w are wider than other lower-case letters. Likewise, I and J and i, l and f are narrower than normal. It is also obvious that capital letters in general are wider than small letters. These differences are recognized in the unit-count system.

Here is how the system works:

When a headline is set in upper and lower case, that is, in capital letters and small letters, the lower-case letters are generally counted as one unit each, except for m and w, which are counted as one and a half units each, and i, l, t and, in some styles of type, f, which are counted as half a unit each. The upper-case letters are counted as one and a half units each, with these exceptions: M and W are counted as two units each, I and J as one unit each. Figures, which are about the same size as capital letters are counted as a unit and a half each, except for the figure 1, which is counted as a single unit. Most punctuation marks are considered to be a half unit each. Naturally, spaces between words must be included in the line count and they are arbitrarily set down as half units even though in the actual setting of the line they may be wider or narrower.

When a headline is set entirely in capital letters the system is even simpler. All letters except the M, W and I are counted as one unit each—M and W, of course, are counted as a unit and a half each and I as half a unit. All figures are counted as a unit each, except 1, which is counted as a half unit. Punctuation marks and spaces between words are counted as a half unit each.

That is all there is to the copy editor's magic key for making lines fit. Thus equipped he can enter any newspaper office, get a headline schedule, determine the maximum counts for the lines of the various heads and be prepared to write headlines that are satisfactory, typographically.

Let us try counting a headline in upper- and lower-case letters to put the system into practice. Here is the head:

Fliers Join
Sham War

And here is how it is counted:

	F	l	i	e	r	s		J	o	i	n	
Count	1½	½	½	1	1	1	½	1	1	½	1	=9½

	S	h	a	m		W	a	r	
Count	1½	1	1	1½	½	2	1	1	=9½

Now let us try a headline made up entirely of capital letters:

1,500 MEN FIGHT
ARMY SHAM WAR

Here is how it is counted:

	1	,	5	0	0		M	E	N		F	I	G	H	T	
Count	½	½	1	1	1	½	1½	1	1	½	1	½	1	1	1	=13

	A	R	M	Y		S	H	A	M		W	A	R	
Count	1	1	1½	1	½	1	1	1	1½	½	1½	1	1	=13½

"BROKEN" AND SHORT HEADLINES

The important thing a copy editor wants to know about a headline he has never tried to write before is the maximum count for each line. For he knows he dare not exceed this limit even by so much as a half unit. If he does exceed it, the headline will "break." And a "broken" headline, that is, one that is too long to fit within the allotted bounds, is a cardinal sin in headline writing, because it cannot be used in the paper and must be rewritten, usually by a make-up man and often hastily at the moment of going to press.

While the minimum count is not so rigid as the maximum, it, too, is important because of the extremely unpleasing typographical effect that results if the lines are too short. Note the poor appearance of the following head:

MEN TO HOLD
SHAM WAR

The importance of the appearance of the headline must not be minimized. Our sample tube of tooth paste is never soiled or partly folded up or encased in a torn box. Neither must the headline look skimpy or crowded or asymmetrical. If an inverted pyramid is called for, it should converge evenly from the top. If drop lines are being written, they should balance—the steps at both ends should be equal. Balance is achieved of course, by writing lines of equal length. The lines need not be of precisely the same length, but they should be within, say, a unit of equal length. If there is too great a discrepancy between the lengths of the lines, again unpleasing effects result, as the following heads illustrate:

MEN FIGHT
SHAM WAR TODAY

1,500 MEN TO JOIN
SHAM WAR

In the bank of a head the copy editor has a little more leeway. Since the count is rarely given in terms of lines that fill the column completely from rule to rule, the copy editor can usually slightly exceed the count that is given without danger of a "break." As a matter of fact, the count specified for banks is usually only an approximation and most often is set forth as a count by letters or even by words, rather than by units. Nevertheless, of course, there are limits even for banks.

The headline writer, then, is engaged in a sort of word game in which he is trying not only to make big ideas fit into little spaces, but also to dress them in pretty clothes. His wits are constantly being challenged by the ever-present bogey of Maximum Count, and to win out he must be in command of armies of short, pithy words and hosts of synonyms. When one word fails him, he must be prepared to throw another or a whole phrase into the breach. In addition, his battles must be won quickly for he has many to wage before he reaches deadline.

His problem, however, is obviously not merely one of getting words to fit, but of getting suitably short words that say the right thing. He is dealing with ideas as well as with words. And since the function of words is always to communicate ideas, what the headline says transcends every other element of it. It is to this subject that we are now ready to turn.

8. WHAT THE HEADLINE SAYS

A HANDFUL of bouillon cubes represents a comparatively large pot of soup in compact form—all that is lacking is the water, which is its bulkiest part, but the essence is there. Similarly, a headline containing a few words gives a handy condensation of a news story that is a stick, half a column or eight columns long. In each case it is a question of boiling down to the essentials.

The top of the headline contains the main highlight of the story. Since it is the most conspicuous part and the part that is read first, the copy editor must present the essence of the news there before he goes further. And it makes no difference whether the top is an eight-column line of 120 point type followed by two or three banks, or whether it is a single line of boldface agate with no banks at all—the top tells the story. The banks and crosslines, if any, elaborate and add facts.

In presenting the kernel of the news, the top must tell the story at hand and tell no other. This is another way of saying it must be specific. Headline space is too precious to be wasted on vague words and generalities.

To illustrate what is meant by a headline's telling one story and no other, let us suppose that an article coming to the copy desk recounts that a banker, who had parked his automobile on a hill without setting the brake, was standing in front of it when the car rolled, knocking him down and slightly injuring him.

The beginner might be tempted to write as his headline: "Man Is Injured by Automobile." The head certainly could not be attacked on the ground of accuracy. There is nothing in it that is wrong. On the other hand, there is not enough in it that is right. It must be remembered that in any urban community men are injured by automobiles by the dozens, so that the foregoing headline might apply to any one of several stories. It does not tell one story and no other. It is too general.

A "nose for news" is every bit as necessary in a copy editor as it is in a reporter. What the copy editor must ask himself about every story that comes before him is: "What is the news in this story? What makes it different from other stories?" Only in that way can he make his headlines appear fresh and interesting. What, then, makes our automobile story different from the general run? Obviously it is the fact that a man was run over, not by someone else's automobile, as is usually the case, but by his own. How much better it would be to write as the head: "Banker Run Over By His Own Auto." Incidentally, we have made our headline more specific by particularizing "banker" instead of generalizing "man."

DISCOVERING THE NEWS

How does the copy editor go about writing headlines? It is imperative that he first edit the copy. This sort of close reading fixes the facts in his mind and gives him time to digest them. But there is another reason why the copy must be edited first. If the copy editor writes the headline at the outset, he may later find, on editing the story, that he is compelled for one reason or another to eliminate or alter facts that he has already included in the head. This necessitates patching up the head and means extra work and loss of time. It is decidedly unworkmanlike and unprofessional to attempt to write the headline before the copy has been edited.

Once the story is in final shape the copy editor sets out to determine its salient point—the point he is to include in the top of the head. He does this by mentally stripping the story of its unimportant details and piercing its comparatively copious verbiage to discover its fundamentals. What does this story really mean? In what would the reader be chiefly interested? What makes the story different? These are the questions that lead him to the point.

The kernel of the news is not always to be found in the lead, because sometimes reporters do not recognize it themselves. The copy editor must always exercise independent judgment on the story. He must be able to discover the news where the reporter, perhaps because he is too close to the story or because his perception is faulty, has overlooked it. In addition to good judgment, the copy editor should, of course, have a complete background of the current news so that he can tell promptly what is fresh and what has been told before, what is important and what is trivial.

If the news is buried too far down in the story, it is the copy editor's duty either to reorganize the copy so as to give it more prominence or to suggest that the story be rewritten. But in any case he must discover what the outstanding point is.

Usually this news point can be phrased in one short sentence. That is what the seasoned copy editor does, consciously or unconsciously, preparatory to writing the head. It is a good plan for the beginner to frame this sentence either mentally or on paper. The sentence will be too long, of course, to be fitted into a headline, but it will form a good working basis and will leave the mind unencumbered by nonessentials.

Let us see how this plan works out. Suppose we are required to put a single-line head, with a maximum count of thirty units, on the following story:

BORDEAUX, France, Nov. 23—Live perch rained from the sky when a waterspout broke over Bordeaux Saturday. The downpour lasted less than thirty seconds, but so many fish fell that motor cars were halted. Housewives gathered up the fish in baskets and basins.

Interesting though the facts of this story are, we obviously cannot include them all in a single-line head. We must, therefore, select the outstanding ones and eliminate those that are subordinate. The important and unusual information in the story is that "live perch rained from the sky during a waterspout at Bordeaux." This, then, is our "news point sentence" that will form the basis of the headline. The task now is simply one of paring the thought down to thirty units.

Eliminating articles and turning the sentence into the present tense—headlines, it will be remembered, employ the present tense to refer to past action—we have: "Live perch rain from sky during waterspout at Bordeaux." This is still much too long, however, and we shall have to do some drastic cutting. Suppose we eliminate the waterspout idea. "Live perch rain from sky at Bordeaux." This line, we find; counts 32½, or 2½ units too much, but we are now within striking distance of the headline. The problem now is not to cut out precisely 2½ units and make the count exactly 30, but to reduce it so that it will be 30 or under. The word "live" seems to be the most likely victim, so let us discard that. Then in polishing the head we may decide that the word "perch" is not quickly understandable, and so we make it "fish."

FISH RAIN FROM SKY AT BORDEAUX

The count is 27, well within the maximum, yet not too short. The headline covers the important and unusual angle of the story. And it attracts and informs the reader. In short, it fills every requirement.

WRITING A TOP AND A BANK

In the foregoing story the headline point was readily apparent, and in the head it was necessary simply to set it down and let it go at that; we had no room for elaboration. Let us now turn to a story that is a little more complex and for which we are called upon to write a headline consisting of a top and a bank. We will assume that the top is to consist of two drop lines of capital letters with a maximum count of 18 units each, and the bank is to be an inverted pyramid of three lines in which the first line has a count of 28 letters (not units this time) and the two other lines call for counts proportionately shorter.

Here is the story:

What is described by builders and railroad men as a "remarkable engineering feat, in many ways unique," will be carried out soon, it was disclosed yesterday by the New York Central Railroad Company, in the construction of a new viaduct as part of the $150,000,000 west side improvement project.

The railroad intends to bore through the Bell Telephone laboratory building at Bethune and Washington Streets and lay its double tracks through the building between the second and fifth floors without disturbing the laboratory equipment and delicate instruments housed in the eleven story structure.

To carry out this plan the New York Central has purchased from the telephone company perpetual rights to air space along the Washington Street frontage of the building. The railroad has contracted to build the foundations and enclose the viaduct in such manner that trains will not disturb the workers or their instruments.

Sound deadening materials will be used in the walls enclosing the viaduct and the tracks will be laid so that vibrations will not be transmitted.

Since the first paragraph is the most natural place to look for the news point, let us examine it. If we boiled it down to a news point sentence we should get something like this: "New York Central Railroad will perform a remarkable engineering feat." A headline built on this sentence, however, would smack of the caption of Civil War days: "Remarkable Engineering Feat." Even an exclamation point would not help it. It would be a case of calling names instead of making a statement. The head would not be informative. We shall have to look further then for our news point.

What we want to tell the reader in this headline is something of the nature of this "remarkable engineering feat." The second paragraph discloses this, and from it we can frame a news point sentence somewhat as follows: "New York Central Railroad will bore through the Bell Telephone laboratory building without disturbing the delicate instruments in it." Fitting all this information into our two drop lines is a large order, but is it necessary to get it all in? For a railroad to tunnel through a building is a striking feat in itself and we may safely concentrate on that one point for the top of the head.

The cat is now out of the bag. In trying to get at "what the story really means," we have hit upon an acceptable phraseology for the head in the sentence just above: "Railroad to tunnel through a building." Writing it out in two lines we find that the first, "railroad to tunnel," counts 16½ units, while the second, "through a building," counts 16. Since our maximum is 18 units for each, the lines will fit easily. We are now ready to write the bank.

It must be remembered that the function of the bank is not

to repeat in different words what has been said before. Rather its object is to elaborate and add facts. Taking the case at hand, we might be tempted to write the bank as follows:

NEW YORK CENTRAL PLANS TO BORE
THROUGH STRUCTURE TO
LAY ITS TRACKS

While it is true that the top is thus elaborated in one particular, identification of the railroad, the rest is merely a paraphrase of the top. The copy editor must constantly bear in mind that what is expected of him is not simply to write words —any words—that will fit and give a pleasing typographical appearance; the headline is expected to be informative.

Two obvious points of elaboration are needed in this bank— identification of the railroad and of the building. And at least one point of added information should find a place in the deck —the fact that the engineering project will not disturb delicate instruments in the building, a fact that we included in our news point sentence, but were forced to crowd out of the top. When all this has been squeezed into the bank the completed head might read as follows:

RAILROAD TO TUNNEL
THROUGH A BUILDING

New York Central to Pierce
Phone Laboratory Without
Jarring Equipment

When the head contains more than one bank, a greater degree of organization of the facts to be apportioned among the several parts is necessary, so that the important ones may receive a proper display and the less significant ones may be relegated to the less conspicuous parts of the headline. Let us try next a four-part head consisting of a top of two drop lines with a maximum count of 15 units each, a first bank in the form of an inverted pyramid with a count of 22 letters in the first line, a crossline of 21 units and a last bank, also in inverted pyramid form, with a count of 22 letters in the first line.

The following is the story for which we are to write the head:

A gaunt gray fox, brought many years ago from the Western plains to a cage in the Bronx Park Zoo, clawed and bit one of a group of small boys yesterday afternoon. The child had inserted his right hand trustingly between the bars to offer the animal a morsel of food. The boy, Herbert Bloomgold, 5 years old, of 765 Garden Street, was rushed to Fordham Hospital, his right forearm badly clawed and the little finger of his right hand fractured.

Unnoticed by park employees, the boys had scrambled over a barrier of rocks right up to the bars, which at the rear of the cage are not screened.

The fox was coaxed to the bars and the Bloomgold boy inserted his hand. The animal snapped its jaws, catching the lad's finger, and thrust a paw through the bars, digging its claws into the arm.

Two park employes, Andrew Mergner and Edward Fury, heard the boy's screams, ran to his assistance and freed him. At the hospital after the wounds had been dressed the boy received an injection to prevent rabies.

There should be little difficulty in framing the news point sentence for this story. It would read about like this: "A fox in the Bronx Zoo clawed and bit a 5-year-old boy who offered it food." Reducing the sentence to headline dimensions, the copy editor might write as the top: "Fox Bites Boy, 5, at the Bronx Zoo." This assuredly tells what happened, but it seems to leave something to be desired. For one thing, we get a slight suspicion that the second line—"at the Bronx Zoo"—is mere "padding," that the words were put there more to fill out the line than for any other reason. For another thing, the story has a "human interest" touch that is omitted from the head and would without doubt greatly improve it if included. This is the boy's trusting offer of food that resulted in the accident —the "biting-the-feeding-hand" motif. Why not, therefore, make an effort to find room for this angle in the top? If we could in some way include the zoo idea in the first line, we should have the second line available for the human interest information. How about "Fox in Zoo Bites Boy, 5"? Too long. "Fox in Zoo Bites Boy." Still too long. "Zoo Fox Bites Boy." This line is 15 units and hence will just fit. Now we are ready for the second line: "Offering It Food." This counts 14 units and is probably satisfactory from the point of view of appearance, but there is ground for one slight objection. To the reader who takes in the head at a glance there might be some ambiguity as to which noun is referred to by the participle "offering." Perhaps this objection is hypercritical, but it would be better to phrase the head so as to preclude any possibility of misunderstanding; so that the meaning is apparent instantly. The line could be written, "Who Offers Food." This permits no uncertainty and incidentally we find that it counts 14½ units and therefore balances our first line nicely. Thus we have the top:

ZOO FOX BITES BOY
WHO OFFERS FOOD

ORGANIZING THE FACTS

With the top of the headline out of the way, the next step is to organize the remaining facts for the rest of the head and the following principles may be laid down:

The first bank elaborates the top and adds the next most important facts after those included in the top.

The crossline sets forth a striking and important subordinate fact.

The last bank finishes off the head with whatever information of value remains.

To apply these principles practically, the copy editor surveys the facts left over after the top has been written and notes the best ones for use in the first bank, but at the same time reserving one good one for the crossline. He then proceeds to write the various parts of the head in the order in which they occur. He never should write the crossline before he has completed the first bank, nor should he proceed to the last bank until the crossline is safely out of the way. This *modus operandi* is necessary in order to avoid awkward repetitions of words and sentence structures, and to insure the proper grammatical organization of the head—points that will be taken up in the next chapter.

Marshaling the facts of our fox story, we note that the animal snapped at the boy and clawed him through the bars and that the boy's finger was fractured. Since the fracture of the finger gives the reader a clue to how much damage was done and demonstrates vividly the power of this wild beast, it would make a striking point for the crossline. Let us therefore reserve this fact and use others for the first bank.

Was there anything in our news point sentence that was crowded out of the top? Two items: identification of the zoo as the one in the Bronx, and the boy's age. These facts, then, should find place in the first bank as items that elaborate the top. The beginner might think of setting them down bluntly somewhat as follows: "It happened in Bronx Park and the boy's age is 5." But the experienced copy editor is not so wasteful of words; he inserts such facts more economically, including them incidentally while he conveys his additional information to the reader. He would probably write:

Animal in Bronx Park Snaps
at Hand Thrust Into Cage
and Claws Child, 5

That seems to cover the points apportioned to the first bank and we may now go on to the crossline. Since the space restrictions of the crossline are rigid like those of the top, it would be well to frame another news point sentence as a basis for it. The count, remember, is to be 21 units. The sentence might be made to read: "The fox fractured one of the boy's fingers with its jaws." The word "fox" is superfluous, since we have it in the top and since the word "animal" is the subject of the first bank. We could therefore begin the crossline with a verb and there would be no doubt as to the subject. Well, then: "Fractures Child's Finger." But the count is 21½ units, ½ too much, and an excess of half a unit is no less impossible for the printer to fit into the line than is one of ten units. Moreover, as we have the word "child" in the first bank, let us avoid repeating it. The line may be remedied as follows: "Fractures Lad's Finger." Now the count is 20 units, which will slip nicely into the space.

The last bank, in addition to rounding up the remaining information, may also elaborate the crossline if this is necessary. Perhaps in this case it would be well to tell what other injury the boy received. What else is left? Two park employes heard the boy's screams, ran to the spot and set him free. The bank, then, might be written as follows:

Arm Lacerated—Cries Bring
Two Attendants on Run
and They Free Him

Here is how the completed headline would look:

ZOO FOX BITES BOY
WHO OFFERS FOOD

Animal in Bronx Park Snaps
at Hand Thrust Into Cage
and Claws Child, 5

FRACTURES LAD'S FINGER

Arm Lacerated—Cries Bring
Two Attendants on Run
and They Free Him

Note that there is no waste of space in this head. Every part of it is used to give information and the story is covered so completely that the hasty reader can get all the essential facts by merely scanning the headline. That is the principal function of the head: to tell the story.

Most headlines cannot be this complete simply because they do not contain so many parts. Many newspapers use only a single bank in their main heads and many others use none at all. This situation makes it the more imperative that the copy editor pack the most possible information into the lines that are available.

Mention was made in the previous chapter of the kicker that is included in some headlines. When it is not used as a mere departmental heading its function is like that of the bank of a head: it elaborates and adds information to the main head. But it should be borne in mind that despite the fact that it appears at the top of the headline it is a subsidiary element.

It is set in smaller type than the main head and does not catch the reader's attention immediately. Therefore it should never contain the principal news of the story. Moreover, it should not be used for a qualification that is essential to the main head. For example, it would not do to write as the main head, "Jones Guilty of Murder," and write as the small kicker, "District Attorney Alleges." This not only would be misleading but also would border on dishonesty.

BULKY, COMPLEX STORIES

If all news articles were as simple and direct as those already used as illustrations, the copy editor's task would be far simpler than it is. But he is constantly confronted with more abstract and, at the same time, more complicated stories which he is expected to compress into a few words. Not infrequently, for example, is he called upon to take some message that it required a statesman or a clergyman days to prepare, thousands of words to convey and hours to deliver, and reproduce the gist of it in half a dozen words within ten minutes. Many stories by their sheer bulk almost overwhelm the copy editor, so that he hardly knows where to begin his job of compression. Stories that contain too much information and too many good news points are one of his tribulations.

An elephant is big, and so is a swarm of locusts. Yet the methods employed to kill them are entirely different. The elephant is most readily dispatched by sending a steel-jacketed bullet into a vital part—the brain, for example. But the same method would hardly be efficient in the case of the locusts—imagine the farmer sitting on a fence, rifle in hand, sniping away at individual insects! One of the most efficacious means of killing off the pests is to blanket them with insecticide.

These two methods illustrate how the copy editor goes

about bringing down the big ones. Bulky stories may be roughly classified as of either the elephant or the locust type. In the case of elephant stories, where there are several good news points of approximately coordinate interest and importance for which no common denominator can be found, the copy editor trains his gun on a vital spot and bags the story with a single shot. In the case of locust stories, where several good news points can be lumped together because they contain some common factor, the copy editor writes a headline that blankets the story.

Conventions of various kinds furnish the majority of these two types of stories. Forums in which many different subjects are taken up would usually be of the elephant classification, while symposiums on a single subject would often be of the locust kind. But these groupings are by no means invariable. A symposium on a single subject frequently could be treated as an elephant story, with better results in the headline.

The Elephant Type. To make clear the distinction between the two types of stories, let us examine an example of each. The following is the beginning of one of the stories:

WASHINGTON, Oct. 5—Protective measures to minimize hazards in traffic, ranging from blind flying to automobile accidents, were discussed today during the third day's sessions of the Annual Safety Congress of the National Safety Council.

To illustrate up-to-date police methods of dealing with motor car accidents, a real collision between automobiles was staged, including the taking of photographs by the traffic officer as well as statements from witnesses.

A better spirit of cooperation in the direction of true highway safety among motorists, drivers and owners of commercial motor vehicles and State regulating agencies was urged by Joseph G. Jones, Commissioner of Motor Vehicles of New Jersey.

Harold P. Smith, president of Metropolitan Airlines, told the meeting of the Safety Council's aeronautical section that the safety record of aviation in this country was an achievement worthy of the highest commendation.

Here several points are presented, too many to be handled easily in a headline. Nor can the copy editor find any generalization to put into the headline that will not be too dull to do the story justice. He therefore treats the story as of the elephant type and shoots at a vital spot. He writes the head as follows:

CAR CRASH STAGED
FOR SAFETY FORUM

The Locust Type. The other story used for purposes of illustration concerns a conference of major industries held at Columbia University, at which twelve speakers from various countries proposed international business agreements for the stimulation of trade and, incidentally, for the furtherance of world peace. A spokesman for Germany advocated a shipping compact; a French automobile manufacturer suggested an international automobile cartel; the president of Columbia University emphasized the international character of the world's economic problems; a representative of Great Britain appealed for cooperation among nations, and so forth.

Almost any one of the addresses would make a meaty story in itself, but they are all fused into a single article. To build the headline on one speech would not give the reader a proper idea of the scope of the conference, nor would it afford the other addresses the treatment they deserve. Here, then, is the locust type of story and the best kind of head to write for it is one that blankets it. This is a possible head:

12 LEADERS URGE NATIONS TO SPUR TRADE AND PEACE

This headline is general enough to encompass the whole story, yet not too vague. It illustrates what can be done if the copy editor can find a common denominator.

Pigmy Elephants. All elephants are not big, nor are all stories that fall into the elephant classification freighted with important facts. On the contrary, some elephant stories are distinctly of the pigmy variety; they contain a succession of comparatively insignificant facts all seeming to be on a dead level. In such cases, although a vital spot may be difficult to find, the copy editor uses a rifle rather than a spray gun, and hence the stories must be classed as the elephant type.

The vital spot may be an unusual quotation or a striking thought. A "headline phrase" or a "headline word" is what the copy editor seeks. He resists to the utmost the temptation to compose a routine headline that these stories customarily offer.

Some years ago an Italian Foreign Minister visited the United States, and while he was here the newspapers tried to report the daily doings of his wife. But she refused interviews and at all times avoided the limelight. The result was trivial copy, little more than a time-table of her goings and comings. In one story it was recorded that the Signora went on a shopping tour to buy gifts for her friends and children. After having visited several stores she went to the toy department of a shop that was gay with Christmas decorations. She gazed around delightedly and exclaimed: "These toys are very charming." Then she bought a little breakfast set for each of her two children, a mechanical army tank for her little boy and two dolls for her little girl. The rest of her day was routine.

Vital points are hard to find in a story like this. But the alert copy editor notes that this woman who had granted no interviews did at last say something that could be quoted. He therefore seizes his rifle, takes aim, pulls the trigger, and presto:

OUR TOYS 'CHARMING'
TO VISITING SIGNORA

And a pigmy elephant has bitten the dust!

Annual reports of institutions and speeches on normally uninteresting subjects—in short, stories that are printed more as a matter of record than as a matter of interest—form the most likely stamping grounds for pigmy elephants, and the copy editor should constantly be on the watch for them to avoid writing dull headlines.

Elephant stories far outnumber locust stories and in all cases where a clear-cut news point is lacking the copy editor will do well to assume that the article is of the elephant type until he has proved it to his own satisfaction to be otherwise. For the attempt to blanket a story in the head is too often likely to produce generalities and vagueness.

It has been noted before that headline space is too precious to be wasted on generalities. The injunction to be imprinted on the copy editor's big black pencil is "Be specific!" From one point of view this requires telling one story and no other, as already indicated. From another, it demands the technique of the elephant story—picking out a salient point rather than indulging in a sweeping statement. But in addition it involves packing the headline with precise facts and figures.

If it is a budget story that is under consideration, the phrase "Big Budget" is not nearly so good as "$52,000,000 Budget"; if it is a robbery story "Valuable Jewelry" is inferior to "$23,000 in Jewelry"; if it is a wreck story "Train Accident" is far less satisfactory than "Train Is Derailed." In each of these examples the inferior form makes a characterization that the reader could deduce for himself from the specific information that the better form sets forth. If "$52,000,000 Budget" is stated, the reader knows it is a "big" budget and receives additional information as to the amount; if he reads "Train Is Derailed" he gets all the information that "Train Accident" would give him and more besides.

Compare the following two headlines from the point of view of the information they convey:

MANY ARE KILLED IN A BUS SMASH-UP	15 WOMEN KILLED AS BUS RAMS POLE

These two headlines have about the same unit count, yet the one on the right contains three more items of information than the one on the left. It tells that "women" were killed, it specifies "15" of them and it reveals how the accident happened: "Bus Rams Pole."

THINGS TO AVOID

Editorializing. The border line between making characterizations—such as "Big Budget"—and editorializing is not always clearly defined. For instance, suppose the headline referred to a "High Budget." The copy editor would leave himself open to a charge of expressing an opinion instead of stating a fact. The question would involve what interpretation would be placed on the word "high" and, although the copy editor might protest that he meant merely "big," others might get the impression he meant excessive. There is no provision for explanatory footnotes, and so the headline must say clearly what it means.

Whereas characterization suffers simply from inadequacy, editorializing is undesirable because it does not adhere to the facts and may easily lend itself to coloring of the news. Opinions are as much out of place in the headline as they are in the news story—there is only one place for them and that is on the editorial page. The headline must reproduce only what is contained in the story; it must say just what the story says.

John Jones, we will suppose, tells the local Ladies' Aid Society in a speech that "the United States is going to the dogs." Our reporter writes his story with this as the lead. Perhaps the copy editor finds it difficult to fit both Jones and the United States into the headline and so he throws up his hands and writes:

UNITED STATES
IS GOING TO DOGS

This is an example of a headline that does not say what the story said. The story recounted that John Jones had said "the United States is going to the dogs." The headline says flatly on its own account that the United States is in this unfortunate condition. It is not a news headline; it is an editorial in display type. The beginner always has a ready solution for this problem.

"I'll put quotation marks around it," he says.

That, however, is not a solution; it is a makeshift; it is an attempt to patch up bad work. Assuming that the reader pays any attention to the quotation marks—and there is no assurance that he will notice them—he still will be in doubt as to their purpose. The quotation marks will not themselves indicate that a speaker or writer is making the statement; for all the reader knows they may indicate merely that the quoted words constitute an editorial slogan of *The Daily Bugle*.

The headline must definitely indicate that someone is responsible for the statement. Either we must get Jones's name into the headline or, if this is not practicable or if the name is not sufficiently well known to justify its use, we must include some verb that will leave no doubt that someone other than *The Bugle* is making the declaration. Here are two possibilities:

JONES SAYS NATION
IS GOING TO DOGS

NATION IS VIEWED
AS GOING TO DOGS

Libel. Saying in the headline exactly what is said in the story is also a foolproof way of avoiding libel, if we assume that the story has been so edited as to free it from committing this offense. Libelous headlines usually arise from the overlooking or ignoring of qualifying facts in the story.

Just as a fair and true account of proceedings in a court of record is privileged from the point of view of libel, so a headline that summarizes this account fairly and accurately is not libelous. If a witness in a proceeding calls Brown a forger, the reporter does not write bluntly: "Brown is a forger," nor even "Brown was revealed as a forger." He writes, "The witness testified that Brown was a forger," or "The witness accused Brown of forgery." Similarly, the headline in reproducing these facts does not say, "Brown Is Forger," or "Brown Revealed as a Forger." It says "Witness Accuses Brown of Forgery," or "Witness Terms Brown a Forger."

There is a difference between saying "Robber Is Held" and "Man Held as Robber." In the first case the headline brands the prisoner as a robber before he has been tried. In the second case it merely reports the charge that has been lodged against him without attempting to indicate whether he is guilty or innocent.

In general it must be remembered that space restrictions of headlines are no defense against libel. If anything, greater care should be taken to guard against libel in writing heads than in writing stories, although this is by no means intended to countenance any laxity on the part of a reporter. The headline gives statements greater prominence than does the story and, since it is inevitably read by more persons, the libel is aggravated, actually if not legally.

So, in addition to being informative and specific, the headline must take no liberties with the facts in the story; it must say just what the story says.

Thus far we have described the size and nature of the cubicle in which the copy editor performs his difficult juggling feats and we have discussed the material he is called upon to juggle. If that were all, it would still be a good trick. But there is more. We are now ready to take up further restrictions he is expected to meet and the methods he employs in keeping his gleaming words and ideas spinning in air.

9. HOW THE HEADLINE SAYS IT

STRICTLY SPEAKING there are only two rules for writing a headline: it must fit and it must tell the story. A head that does not fit is of no use at all, and one that does not tell the story is useful only in a decorative way.

But while there are only two rules, many customs, usages and guides that have persisted because sound reasons underlie them have acquired almost the force of rules. Although it must be borne in mind that they are not inflexible, that in extreme cases they are subordinated to the two rules, the best headlines comply with them.

THE ALL-IMPORTANT VERB

It has been noted that a headline is distinguished from a caption by the fact that it makes a statement instead of merely labeling. It has been further pointed out that the key to this distinction is the presence of a verb in the headline. We may therefore take it as one of our first guides that every part of a headline should contain a verb.

The headline verb may be either explicit or implied. The previously cited head, "Our Toys 'Charming' to Visiting Signora," for example, contains the implied verb "are." The word order frequently decides between a mere label and a statement containing an implied verb. Compare, for instance, "Victorious Troops" to "Troops Victorious."

Not only should the head contain a verb, but in the top it is considered preferable to put the verb in the very first line. Since the first line is the one that gives the reader his initial impression of the story when the head is seen at a glance, it should, if possible, be more than just a label line. When it contains a subject and a predicate, while it may not make a complete statement, it at least provides an excellent start for one. "Fox in Zoo Bites" conveys more information and gives a better start to a statement than "Fox in Bronx Zoo." In the latter instance the reader must go on to the next line to get a clue to the nature of the story.

Perhaps it seems a small point to distinguish thus between successive lines in the top, but it must be remembered that one aim of the head is to inform quickly and any device, such as the one just discussed, that serves this end is valuable. Carrying this idea still further, the head strives to set forth in the first line at least one of the elements that "make the story," something that identifies the subject matter instantly. When feasible, the "blind" top line should be avoided. The following heads illustrate the point:

DEATH CLAIMS TWO IN AUTO CRASH	TWO DIE IN CRASH AS AUTO HITS BUS

The head on the left fills the requirement for a verb in the first line, but the line is blind. The reader must go to the second line to find the element that makes the story. In the head on the right, however, all the news is in the first line—it can be seen instantly.

Whatever the story, the copy editor should try to make the first line of the head a telling one, to insert a verb that sets it in motion and to include an identifying element.

Besides informing quickly, the headline, as noted previously, tries to deliver its message in attractive style. It seeks to be forceful, colorful, active. While in ordinary writing such qualities may be achieved partly by well-selected adjectives, in headlines there is usually little space to spare for these parts of speech. Here again the verb is all-important. A well-chosen, potent verb can suffuse the head with energy; a flat, colorless one leaves it limp and lifeless. The verb determines whether the headline contains "punch" or is dull.

Facts must under no circumstances be strained or exaggerated for the sake of using a forceful verb, but when the news itself is dynamic it is a mistake to employ any but a forceful verb. If a liner comes into port after a stormy voyage, with railings torn loose by dashing waves and ports smashed by pounding seas, it is inadequate to say in the head, "Liner Reports Storm at Sea." A more attractive and at the same time more informative head might be: "Liner Battered by Heavy Seas." The verb in this case pictures the story and gives animation to the head; the lines would be more likely to tempt the reader than would the other head, which merely records the fact that a ship encountered a storm.

Too much emphasis cannot be laid upon the necessity for choosing strong verbs and avoiding weak ones, for the verb more than any other factor is the key to a successful headline. In general it is well to shun parts of the verbs "to be" and "to have" as the principal verbs in heads; these two are the most obvious of the weaklings. Note in the following illustrations how headlines are brightened by replacing these weak verbs with stronger ones:

JONES IS NEW MAYOR
JONES WINS MAYORALTY

CHILE HAS A GALE
GALE LASHES CHILE

If we are trying to achieve vigor in heads through verbs, it follows that the active voice is to be preferred to the passive voice. And the copy editor takes cognizance of this, using active verbs whenever practicable. This suggestion, however, is qualified by the previous one that calls for including the important news element in the first line. If using the active voice necessitates dropping this element to the second line, it is better to reverse the order of the head and sacrifice telling the story actively to telling it quickly. Taking as an example an injury to Governor Jones of New York during a tour of the West, we might compose either of the following heads:

AUTO CRASH INJURES GOV. JONES IN WEST	GOV. JONES INJURED IN CRASH IN THE WEST

The one on the left employs the active voice but the one on the right puts the important news into the first line, telling the reader quickly what he wants to know. "Gov. Jones Injured" is, therefore, the preferable line.

FIGURATIVE WORDS AND CONSTRUCTIONS

Words are frequently used in a figurative or semifigurative sense to lend color to a headline, and this is good practice provided the figurative uses are not too hackneyed or do not exaggerate the facts. When a speaker opposes a project it is proper to say he "attacks" it if his opposition is really that strong. If a man merely casts a negative vote on a project it would be an exaggeration to say he "attacks" it. More will be said later about the use of "headline words." What is to be noted at this point is that figurative words, properly used, are among the legitimate ornaments the copy editor employs to make the headline more attractive.

Likewise figures of speech have their place as valuable adornments, but they too must be used with discretion. Improperly used, they may prove either ambiguous or ridiculous. Here is an example of a metaphorical structure lending strength and interest to a headline that might otherwise be prosaic:

10. A CLINIC FOR AILING HEADLINES

JUST AS the classroom work of the student doctor becomes real when he is confronted with an actual patient, so the student of copy editing may be helped if he is confronted at this point with a group of actual headlines that demonstrate assorted ailments.

A good many of these patients, but not all, exhibit a common symptom—ambiguity. Others suffer from obscurity. There is a remedy for both ambiguity and obscurity, but it is not easy to apply. The copy editor must summon to mind the fact that whereas the story is known to him since he has just read it, it is not known to the newspaper reader. The copy editor therefore must figuratively pull back from the headline he has just written and try to view it afresh, as if he were a reader seeing it for the first time. He must determine whether it will instantly convey meaning to the reader or whether it is just a jumble of words. This treatment will help to cure obscurity. The copy editor must also examine every word and phrase in the head to see whether it is susceptible of a meaning different from the one intended, and in so doing he must assume the reader to be a really perverse fellow. This treatment will help to cure ambiguity. It cannot be overemphasized that if the headline is to serve its purpose it must be clear at first glance.

Let us examine a dozen categories of sick headlines:

1. Two-faced heads. (Double meanings.)

DIVER GETS CROSS
IN ICY RIVER RITE

Why wouldn't he?

U.S. RULES ON TAX
ADOPTED BY STATE

Is "rules" a noun or a verb?

YOUTH OF 80 LANDS
AT RALLY IN INDIA

"Lands" is intended to be a noun, but that is not instantly clear.

LANDLADY ADMITS
SIXTY VIOLATIONS

No comment necessary.

2. Deadheads. (They say nothing.)

PROSECUTION RESTS

What trial is being referred to?

SUPPORT IS REAFFIRMED

Deadheads are produced by lazy or overhasty editors. The cure for this headline malady is simply the injunction set forth in a previous chapter: Be specific. At the very least the headline must contain some word or phrase that identifies the subject matter of the story.

3. Heads that say too much. (They go beyond the facts or overstate them.)

JUDGE SUGGESTS JAIL
FOR UNWED MOTHERS

In the story what the judge suggested was that unwed mothers of three or more children be jailed. He was not proposing to penalize all unwed mothers, as the head suggests, but rather was taking the view that anyone could make a mistake—or two.

PLEVEN TO FORM
CABINET IN PARIS

M. Pleven agreed to try to form a cabinet. The head goes too far in saying flatly that he is going to form one. Actually in this instance the head was proved wrong within forty-eight hours. He failed.

4. *Misleading heads.* (They give a wrong impression.)

RUSSIAN BLOWS
UP AIRLINER

The story said that a Russian who suddenly went berserk exploded a hand grenade aboard a Venezuelan plane causing it to crash. Thus, the head makes no incorrect statement. Still the use of the word "Russian," particularly at a time when the Russians were being troublesome to the West, suggests a story quite different from the one that would be suggested by the word "madman," for instance. Deliberately or inadvertantly, the head is misleading. This is as bad as if it had been incorrect.

250 FLEE FIRE IN SHIP

Fire at Sea? No. It was a forest fire and the 250 were evacuated from the area in a small craft.

5. *Faultily constructed heads.* (Words or phrases out of place.)

NEW DATA FOUND
ON MRS. LINCOLN

Sounds as if she was frisked.

PANACEAS SCORED
FOR DELINQUENCY

What are delinquent panaceas?

SOLDIER SAVES AIRLINER

Lights Army Strip for Plane
Without Any Electricity

It is not immediately clear whether "without any electricity" applies to "lights" or to "plane."

6. *Heads containing ambiguous words.* (Two-faced heads with a special problem.)

LEGISLATOR HURT
IN CRASH IS GRAVE

Some adjectives describing a person's state of health are ambiguous. Here are two headlines that appeared in a single issue of a newspaper:

QUEENS MAN STILL CRITICAL

CANDIDATE IS CRITICAL

The first reported the aftermath of a fall, the second reported a political speech. Some adjectives of this kind are unambiguous—"healthy," "well," "ill," "sick." Others could be ambiguous but usually are not—"better," "improved," "worse." Still others can be, and often are, ambiguous, and these are the ones to watch out for—"grave," "critical," "serious," "fine," "good" and "satisfactory." They should never appear in heads unattended by "condition" or "health" or "doctors find" or something else that dissipates any possible misunderstanding.

7. *Noun-instead-of-adjective heads.*

POLAND REDS CITE
LACK OF WORKERS

Since "Polish" would fit in this head, the use of "Poland" is inexcusable. The use of nouns as adjectives is a normal occurrence in English and should not be ruled out of headlines, as was explained in a previous chapter. But when nouns are used abnormally, as "Poland" is in this headline, the usage is disapproved.

8. Incompletely worded heads. (Words omitted willy-nilly.)

CULTURAL INSTITUTIONS FEARED LEAVING
MORNINGSIDE IF HOUSING STILL LAGS

Although it is permissible in headlines to omit nonessential words, it must be possible by supplying the missing words to obtain a normal, grammatical English sentence. This is not possible in the quoted head.

9. Vague heads. (Too remote from subject.)

ARMS COLLECTOR
DEFENDS OBJECT

This head seems to be about a connoisseur of weapons, a notion that is reinforced by the word "object," which suggests *objet d'art*. In reality the story was about a man charged with establishing an arsenal for the Irish Republican Army, who was defending the goal of his action. The headline writer knew what the story was, but how was the poor reader to guess?

10. Split heads. (Otherwise known as wrap-around heads.)

NIXON AGAIN DECLARES U.S.
MIGHT COULD DETER ATTACK

Normally the split head does not lead to this much discomfort. Here it lends momentary ambiguity to the word "might."

11. Rhymed heads. (They're oh so pat and fall so flat.)

'POET IN WAITING'
BIDS FOR A RATING

The story was about Robert Frost, who assuredly was not given to jingles of that sort. The copy editor might as well make up his mind to it: In trying to achieve poetry in the limited confines of a headline the best he is ever likely to get is doggerel. If that is appropriate (see page 174), fine. Otherwise, no.

Here is a tabloid head that escapes the mediocrity of a mere jingle and would pass—in any tabloid:

MADCAP MAYOR
JAILED, BAILED
AND UNQUAILED

12. Punning heads. (With double-play words.)

PITCHER HAD A FINE SERIES

This was about a baseball player who was fined for unbecoming behavior in the world series.

GIANTS GET BOOT OUT OF CHANDLER

About a punter on the Giants football team. Both heads are very funny, no? No.

Two tests can be propounded for puns, whether in a headline or elsewhere. The first is whether each of the two meanings of the word forming the pun is appropriate. A rather fair pun that meets this test is included in the following head on a story about high school youths who visited shops to study merchandising:

STUDENTS LEARN
WHAT'S IN STORE

The second test is based on the theory that the basis of humor is incongruity and unexpectedness. This means that the pun should not be obvious; it should not be just lying around waiting to be picked up, as it was in each of the first two heads quoted.

Puns that don't come off can be very sad indeed, as the examples show. The best advice that can be given to the headline writer is to avoid the pun unless he is convinced that it is exceptionally good. If there is one thing that most newspapers need, it is more sophistication. The bad pun, like the childish rhyme, is the mortal enemy of this quality.

II. A HEADLINE VOCABULARY OF RELATED WORDS

ONE overwhelming advantage that the experienced headline writer has over the novice is facility in calling to mind synonyms and substitute words when one word is unserviceable because of its length or because of an incorrect shade of meaning. This facility, of course, depends to some extent on the vocabulary of the worker, but to a much larger extent it is the result of practice. Whereas the beginner might fumble for a word for many minutes, the veteran can usually summon one almost instantaneously.

The list of the most common headline words presented herewith was assembled in an attempt to offset in part this handicap. But, in addition, it is hoped that the list will prove valuable to the experienced desk man in speeding up his work and in helping him over those tortuous moments when the required word mischievously eludes him.

A danger that seemed apparent when the idea for this list was conceived was that it would make for undesirable standardization of expression, that it would cause the headline writer to imitate rather than to create. To avoid this as far as possible, the list deliberately excludes all phrases and figures of speech, so that it will not suggest hackneyed headline constructions.

The list is made up of main entries and cross references in simple alphabetical order. Each main entry is a key word and is followed by a group of related words. It should be emphasized that the list is in no sense a dictionary of synonyms, as it includes more than mere synonyms and at the same time disregards those that have no headline utility. Furthermore, words are grouped solely on the basis of the headline ideas they suggest, sometimes making strange but not uncongenial bedfellows.

The main entry, or key word, does not, and is not intended to cover all the meanings of the words in that particular grouping. It is purely arbitrary and was chosen simply because of the general thought it suggests.

An asterisk following a word indicates that the word is viewed with disfavor for headline purposes and would better be avoided altogether or used sparingly.

A

abandon: *see* RESIGN
abandonment: *see* RESIGN
abate: *see* FALL; STOP
abatement: *see* FALL; STOP
abdicate: *see* RESIGN
abdication: *see* RESIGN
abduct: *see* DISAPPEAR
abduction: *see* DISAPPEAR
abet: *see* APPROVAL
abolish: *see* RELIEVE; STOP
abolition: *see* RELIEVE; STOP
absolve: *see* ACQUIT
absorb: *see* ORGANIZATION
ACCIDENT

Verbs

collide
crash
crush
hit
ram
smash
strike

ACCIDENT (*cont.*)

Nouns

catastrophe
collision
crash
disaster
mishap
smash-up
tragedy
wreck

acclaim: *see* APPROVAL
accord: *see* GIVE; PEACE
ACCUSE: *see also* OPPOSITION

Verbs

allege
arraign
ascribe
attribute
blame
charge
cite
credit
denounce

ACCUSE (*cont.*)
implicate
indict
involve
lay
link
name
Nouns
allegation
blame
charge
denunciation
indictment
true bill
acknowledge: *see* ADMIT
acknowledgment: *see* ADMIT
acme: *see* PEAK
acquire: *see* GET
acquisition: *see* GET
ACQUIT
Verbs
absolve
clear
defend
exonerate
free
release
uphold
vindicate
Nouns
acquittal
exoneration
freedom
release
vindication
acquittal: *see* ACQUIT
act: *see* ADVANCE; ORDER; START
action: *see* ADVANCE
add: *see* RISE
addition: *see* RISE
address: *see* SAY
adjust: *see* REVISE
adjustment: *see* REVISE
admission: *see* ADMIT
ADMIT
Verbs

ADMIT (*cont.*)
acknowledge
avow
concede
confess
own
Nouns
acknowledgment
admission
avowal
confession
adopt: *see* APPROVAL
adoption: *see* APPROVAL
ADVANCE
Verbs
act
bring
cause
expedite
facilitate
hasten
impel
press
prod
push
quicken
result
rush
speed
spur
stimulate
stir
Nouns
action
progress
speed
adversary: *see* OPPOSITION
affect: *see* DAMAGE
affirm: *see* SAY
affirmation: *see* SAY
afford: *see* GIVE
agenda: *see* PLAN
agree: *see* PEACE; PLAN; PROMISE
agreement: *see* PEACE; PLAN; PROMISE
aid: *see* APPROVAL; RELIEVE

aim: *see* PLAN
alarm: *see* DANGER
allay: *see* RELIEVE
allegation: *see* ACCUSE; SAY
allege: *see* ACCUSE; SAY
alleviate: *see* RELIEVE
alleviation: *see* RELIEVE
alliance: *see* ORGANIZATION
allocate: *see* GIVE
allocation: *see* GIVE
allot: *see* GIVE
allotment: *see* GIVE
allow: *see* APPROVAL
ally: *see* ORGANIZATION
alter: *see* REVISE
alteration: *see* REVISE
amaze: *see* PUZZLE
amazement: *see* PUZZLE
amend: *see* REVISE
amendment: *see* REVISE
amity: *see* PEACE
analysis: *see* INVESTIGATE
analyze: *see* INVESTIGATE
anger: *see* ANNOY
angry: *see* ANNOY
announce: *see* SHOW
announcement: *see* SHOW
ANNOY: *see also* RIDICULE

Verbs

anger
arouse
awaken
bother
disturb
enrage
fret
harass
harry
irk
irritate
stir
torment
vex

Nouns

anger
disturbance
fury
ire
rage
wrath

Adjectives

angry
irate
wroth

answer: *see* REPLY
anticipate: *see* PREDICT
anticipation: *see* PREDICT
anxiety: *see* DANGER
anxious: *see* DANGER
apartment: *see* BUILDING
apathetic: *see* CALM
apathy: *see* CALM
appeal: *see* REQUEST
applaud: *see* APPROVAL
appoint: *see* CHOOSE
appointment: *see* CHOOSE
apportion: *see* GIVE
apportionment: *see* GIVE
apprehend: *see* ARREST
approach: *see* FACE
APPROVAL: *see also* ADVANCE

Verbs

abet
acclaim
adopt
aid
allow
applaud
approve
ask
assist
authorize
back
commend
confirm
defend
demand
encourage
endorse
espouse
eulogize

APPROVAL (*cont.*)
extol
favor
further
gratify
hail
hearten
help
justify
laud
pass
permit
please
propose
ratify
request
sanction
seek
suggest
support
sustain
uphold
urge
vote
want

Nouns
acclaim
adoption
aid
assistance
authorization
backing
commendation
confirmation
defense
endorsement
eulogy
favor
help
passage
permission
plaudit
ratification
sanction
support

approve: *see* APPROVAL
arbitrate: *see* PEACE
arbitration: *see* PEACE

ARDENT

Nouns
ardor
avidity
cordiality
eagerness
enthusiasm
fervor
joy
zeal

Adjectives
avid
cordial
eager
enthusiastic
fervent
joyful
zealous

ardor: *see* ARDENT

AREA

Nouns
district
locality
neighborhood
place
region
scene
section
site
sphere
tract
vicinity
zone

argue: *see* DISCUSS; OPPOSITION
argument: *see* DISCUSS; OPPOSITION
arise: *see* RISE
armistice: *see* PEACE
arouse: *see* ANNOY
arraign: *see* ACCUSE
arrange: *see* PLAN
arrangement: *see* PEACE; PLAN
array: *see* MEETING

ARREST

Verbs

ARREST (*cont.*)
apprehend
capture
catch
hold
net
round up
seize
take
trap
Nouns
apprehension
capture
round-up
seizure

ascend: *see* RISE
ascension: *see* RISE
ascent: *see* RISE
ascribe: *see* ACCUSE
ask: *see* APPROVAL; QUESTION; REQUEST
aspersion: *see* BELITTLE
assail: *see* OPPOSITION
assault: *see* OPPOSITION
assemblage: *see* MEETING
assemble: *see* MEETING
assembly: *see* MEETING
assert: *see* SAY
assertion: *see* SAY
assess: *see* TAX
assessment: *see* TAX
assist: *see* APPROVAL
assistance: *see* APPROVAL
association: *see* ORGANIZATION
assurance: *see* PROMISE
assure: *see* PROMISE
astonish: *see* PUZZLE
astonishment: *see* PUZZLE
astound: *see* PUZZLE
attack: *see* OPPOSITION
attitude: *see* POLICY
attribute: *see* ACCUSE
augment: *see* RISE
authority: *see* LEADER
authorization: *see* APPROVAL
authorize: *see* APPROVAL
aver: *see* SAY
avert: *see* STOP
avid: *see* ARDENT
avidity: *see* ARDENT
avoid: *see* STOP
avow: *see* ADMIT; SAY
avowal: *see* ADMIT; PROMISE; SAY
awaken: *see* ANNOY
await: *see* FACE
award: *see* GIVE; ORDER
awe: *see* PUZZLE

B

back: *see* APPROVAL
backing: *see* APPROVAL
baffle: *see* PUZZLE
bake: *see* HEAT
balk: *see* PUZZLE; STOP
ban: *see* OPPOSITION; STOP
band: *see* ORGANIZATION
bandit: *see* STEAL
bar: *see* OPPOSITION; STOP
bare: *see* SHOW
bargain: *see* PEACE
barrier: *see* STOP
batter: *see* STORM
battle: *see* OPPOSITION; VIOLENCE
beat: *see* WIN
beg: *see* REQUEST
begin: *see* START
beginning: *see* START
belief: *see* POLICY; SAY
believe: *see* SAY

BELITTLE: *see also* RIDICULE
Verbs
deprecate
depreciate
discount
discredit
disparage
disregard
ignore
malign
minimize
shun
slight

BELITTLE (*cont.*)
slur
spurn
undermine
Nouns
aspersion
disparagement
slight
slur
bequeath: *see* GIVE
bequest: *see* GIVE
berate: *see* OPPOSITION
beseech: *see* REQUEST
best: *see* WIN
bestow: *see* GIVE
bestowal: *see* GIVE
betray: *see* SHOW
better: *see* RELIEVE
betterment: *see* RELIEVE
bewilder: *see* PUZZLE
bewilderment: *see* PUZZLE
BIAS
Verbs
discriminate
favor
prejudice
Nouns
discrimination
favoritism
leaning
prejudice
Adjectives
partial
unfair
bicker: *see* OPPOSITION
bid: *see* ORDER; REQUEST
blame: *see* ACCUSE
blanket: *see* SNOW
blast: *see* COLD
blaze: *see* FIRE
blizzard: *see* SNOW; STORM
block: *see* STOP
blow: *see* OPPOSITION
board: *see* ORGANIZATION
body: *see* ORGANIZATION
bolt: *see* ESCAPE; STORM
bond: *see* ORGANIZATION
boo: *see* RIDICULE
booty: *see* STEAL
bother: *see* ANNOY
bow: *see* LOSE
branch: *see* ORGANIZATION
brand: *see* DESCRIBE
brave: *see* DANGER
brawl: *see* VIOLENCE
breach: *see* OPPOSITION
break: *see* ESCAPE; OPPOSITION; STORM
bring: *see* ADVANCE
broaden: *see* RISE
buffet: *see* STORM
build: *see* BUILDING
BUILDING
Verbs
build
construct
erect
rear
rise
Nouns
apartment
center
edifice
house
institution
plant
skyscraper
structure
tenement
tower
burden: *see* DIFFICULTY; TAX
burglar: *see* STEAL
burglary: *see* STEAL
burn: *see* FIRE
bury: *see* HIDE; SNOW

C

cache: *see* HIDE
call: *see* DESCRIBE
call for: *see* REQUEST
CALM: *see also* PEACE
Verbs

CALM (*cont.*)
hush
quiet
silence
soothe
still
Nouns
apathy
coolness
indifference
inertia
neutrality
quiet
torpor
unconcern
Adjectives
apathetic
cold
cool
firm
indifferent
mum *
mute
neutral
quiet
silent
unconcerned
unmoved

CAMPAIGN: *see also* OPPOSITION
Nouns
course
drive
effort
move
program

cancel: *see* OPPOSITION
cap: *see* PEAK
capture: *see* ARREST
catastrophe: *see* ACCIDENT
catcall: *see* RIDICULE
catch: *see* ARREST
catechize: *see* QUESTION
cause: *see* ADVANCE
caution: *see* DANGER
cease: *see* STOP
cede: *see* GIVE
celebrate: *see* CEREMONY
celebration: *see* CEREMONY
censure: *see* OPPOSITION
center: *see* BUILDING; ORGANIZATION

CEREMONY
Verbs
celebrate
hold
mark
observe
perform
stage
Nouns
celebration
display
event
exercises
fete
observance
pageant
parade
party
performance
procession
review
service
spectacle

chairman: *see* LEADER
challenge: *see* OPPOSITION; QUESTION
change: *see* REVISE
chaos: *see* VIOLENCE
charge: *see* ACCUSE; ORDER; SAY
chart: *see* PLAN
chase: *see* PURSUE
chat: *see* SAY
cheat: *see* STEAL
check: *see* STOP
cheer: *see* GREET; HONOR
chide: *see* OPPOSITION; RIDICULE
chief: *see* LEADER
chill: *see* COLD
choice: *see* CHOOSE
choke: *see* SNOW; STOP

CHOOSE

CHOOSE (*cont.*)
Verbs
appoint
designate
elect
name
nominate
pick
select
Nouns
appointment
choice
designation
election
nomination
selection
cite: *see* ACCUSE; SAY
claim: *see* SAY
clamor: *see* VIOLENCE
clash: *see* OPPOSITION; VIOLENCE
clear: *see* ACQUIT
climax: *see* PEAK
climb: *see* RISE
cloak: *see* HIDE; SNOW
clog: *see* SNOW; STOP
close: *see* STOP
closing: *see* STOP
cloud-burst: *see* STORM
club: *see* ORGANIZATION
clue: *see* DISCOVER
COLD: *see also* CALM
Verbs
chill
freeze
grip
nip
sweep
Nouns
blast
chill
mercury
spell
temperature
thermometer
wave
Adjectives

COLD (*cont.*)
chill
frigid
icy
wintry
collapse: *see* FALL
collide: *see* ACCIDENT
collision: *see* ACCIDENT
combat: *see* OPPOSITION; VIOLENCE
combination: *see* ORGANIZATION
combine: *see* ORGANIZATION
command: *see* LEADER; ORDER
commander: *see* LEADER
commence: *see* START
commend: *see* APPROVAL
commendation: *see* APPROVAL
commission: *see* ORGANIZATION
committee: *see* ORGANIZATION
compact: *see* PEACE
company: *see* ORGANIZATION
COMPARE
Verbs
contrast
liken
link
parallel
Nouns
comparison
contrast
likeness
parallel
comparison: *see* COMPARE
complete: *see* STOP
completion: *see* STOP
conceal: *see* HIDE
concede: *see* ADMIT
concern: *see* DANGER; ORGANIZATION
conciliate: *see* PEACE
conciliation: *see* PEACE
concord: *see* PEACE
condemn: *see* OPPOSITION
condemnation: *see* OPPOSITION
confer: *see* GIVE; MEETING
conference: *see* MEETING
confess: *see* ADMIT
confession: *see* ADMIT

confirm: *see* APPROVAL
confirmation: *see* APPROVAL
conflagration: *see* FIRE
conflict: *see* OPPOSITION; VIOLENCE
confound: *see* PUZZLE
confront: *see* FACE
confuse: *see* PUZZLE
confusion: *see* PUZZLE; VIOLENCE
congratulate: *see* HONOR
congratulation: *see* HONOR
congregate: *see* MEETING
congress: *see* MEETING
conquer: *see* WIN
consider: *see* DISCUSS; SAY
consolidate: *see* ORGANIZATION
conspiracy: *see* PLAN
conspire: *see* PLAN
construct: *see* BUILDING
contend: *see* SAY
contention: *see* SAY
contest: *see* OPPOSITION
contradict: *see* DENY
contradiction: *see* DENY
contrast: *see* COMPARE
contribute: *see* GIVE
contribution: *see* GIVE
control: *see* LEADER; ORDER
controversy: *see* OPPOSITION
convene: *see* MEETING
convention: *see* MEETING
convocation: *see* MEETING
convoke: *see* MEETING
cool: *see* CALM
coolness: *see* CALM
cordial: *see* ARDENT
cordiality: *see* ARDENT
corporation: *see* ORGANIZATION
corps: *see* ORGANIZATION
correct: *see* RELIEVE
correction: *see* RELIEVE
corrective: *see* RELIEVE
course: *see* CAMPAIGN
cover: *see* FLOOD; SNOW
cow: *see* STOP
crash: *see* ACCIDENT
create: *see* START
creation: *see* START
credit: *see* ACCUSE
crest: *see* PEAK
cripple: *see* DAMAGE; STOP
crown: *see* PEAK
crush: *see* ACCIDENT; WIN
curb: *see* STOP
cure: *see* RELIEVE
curtail: *see* STOP
curtailment: *see* STOP
custom: *see* TAX
cut: *see* FALL
cyclone: *see* STORM

D

DAMAGE

Verbs

affect
cripple
destroy
gut *
harm
hurt
impair
injure
level
mar
ravage
raze
ruin
scar
spoil
wreck

Nouns

debris
destruction
harm
hurt
injury
loss
ruin
wreckage

DANGER

Verbs

brave
caution

DANGER (*cont.*)
concern
dare
defend
dread
endanger
fear
frighten
guard
imperil
jeopardize
menace
peril
protect
risk
scent
terrify
terrorize
threaten
trouble
warn
Nouns
alarm
anxiety
caution
concern
fear
flurry
fright
hazard
jeopardy
menace
peril
risk
scare *
tension
terror
threat
trouble
Adjectives
anxious
tense
wary

dare: *see* DANGER
deadlock: *see* STOP
deal: *see* PEACE

DEATH
Verbs
destroy
die
execute
kill
murder
perish
slay
succumb
Nouns
destruction
execution
homicide
killing
manslaughter
murder
slaughter
slaying
suicide

debate: *see* DISCUSS; OPPOSITION
debris: *see* DAMAGE
deceive: *see* STEAL
decide: *see* PLAN; SAY
decision: *see* ORDER
declaration: *see* SAY
declare: *see* SAY
decline: *see* FALL
decrease: *see* FALL
decree: *see* ORDER
decry: *see* OPPOSITION
deem: *see* SAY
defalcate: *see* STEAL
defalcation: *see* STEAL
defeat: *see* LOSE; WIN
defend: *see* ACQUIT; APPROVAL; DANGER
defense: *see* APPROVAL
defer: *see* POSTPONE
defiance: *see* OPPOSITION
deflate: *see* FALL
deflation: *see* FALL
defraud: *see* STEAL
defy: *see* OPPOSITION
delay: *see* POSTPONE
deluge: *see* FLOOD; STORM

delve: *see* INVESTIGATE
demand: *see* APPROVAL; REQUEST
demonstrate: *see* SHOW; VIOLENCE
demonstration: *see* SHOW; VIOLENCE
denial: *see* DENY
denounce: *see* ACCUSE; OPPOSITION
denunciation: *see* ACCUSE; OPPOSITION

DENY

Verbs

contradict
disavow
disclaim
disown
dispute
gainsay
recant
refuse
refute
reject
renounce
repudiate
retract
scout
withhold

Nouns

contradiction
denial
disavowal
disclaimer
refusal
refutation
rejection
renunciation
repudiation
retraction

depart: *see* DISAPPEAR
depict: *see* DESCRIBE
deplore: *see* OPPOSITION
depose: *see* RESIGN
deprecate: *see* BELITTLE
depreciate: *see* BELITTLE
depress: *see* FALL
depression: *see* FALL
deride: *see* RIDICULE
derision: *see* RIDICULE
descend: *see* FALL
descent: *see* FALL

DESCRIBE

Verbs

brand
call
depict
explain
name
narrate
outline
picture
portray
relate
report
style
tell
term

Nouns

description
explanation
narrative
outline
portrayal
report
story
tale

description: *see* DESCRIBE
desert: *see* RESIGN
desertion: *see* RESIGN
design: *see* PLAN
designate: *see* CHOOSE
designation: *see* CHOOSE
desire: *see* REQUEST
destroy: *see* DAMAGE; DEATH
destruction: *see* DAMAGE; DEATH
detect: *see* DISCOVER
detection: *see* DISCOVER
deter: *see* STOP
determine: *see* DISCOVER; PLAN
develop: *see* ORGANIZATION; RISE
dictate: *see* LEADER; ORDER
dictator: *see* LEADER
die: *see* DEATH
differ: *see* OPPOSITION

DIFFICULTY

DIFFICULTY (*cont.*)
Nouns
burden
distress
evil
ill
malady
onus
trouble
woe
dig up: *see* DISCOVER
dim: *see* DISAPPEAR
diminish: *see* FALL
din: *see* VIOLENCE
direct: *see* LEADER; ORDER
director: *see* LEADER
disagree: *see* OPPOSITION
DISAPPEAR
Verbs
abduct
depart
dim
elope
fade
go
kidnap
leave
lose
melt
quit
vanish
Nouns
abduction
disappearance
kidnapping
loss
runaway
Adjectives
gone
missing
disappearance: *see* DISAPPEAR
disapproval: *see* OPPOSITION
disapprove: *see* OPPOSITION
disaster: *see* ACCIDENT
disavow: *see* DENY
disavowal: *see* DENY
discard: *see* OPPOSITION
discern: *see* DISCOVER; SAY
disclaim: *see* DENY
disclaimer: *see* DENY
disclose: *see* SHOW
disclosure: *see* SHOW
discord: *see* OPPOSITION; VIOLENCE
discount: *see* BELITTLE
DISCOVER: *see also* SHOW
Verbs
detect
determine
dig up
discern
ferret
find
solve
unearth
unravel
Nouns
clue
detection
discovery
find
key
lead
solution
discovery: *see* DISCOVER
discredit: *see* BELITTLE
discriminate: *see* BIAS
discrimination: *see* BIAS
DISCUSS
Verbs
argue
consider
debate
take up
weigh
Nouns
argument
debate
discussion
forum
symposium
discussion: *see* DISCUSS
dislike: *see* OPPOSITION

dismiss: *see* RESIGN
dismissal: *see* RESIGN
disorder: *see* VIOLENCE
disown: *see* DENY
disparage: *see* BELITTLE
disparagement: *see* BELITTLE
display: *see* CEREMONY; SHOW
dispute: *see* DENY; OPPOSITION
disregard: *see* BELITTLE
dissension: *see* OPPOSITION
dissent: *see* OPPOSITION
distress: *see* DIFFICULTY
distribute: *see* GIVE
distribution: *see* GIVE
district: *see* AREA
disturb: *see* ANNOY
disturbance: *see* ANNOY; VIOLENCE
dive: *see* FALL
divide: *see* OPPOSITION
division: *see* OPPOSITION
divulge: *see* SHOW
dodge: *see* ESCAPE
donate: *see* GIVE
donation: *see* GIVE
doubt: *see* QUESTION
doubtful: *see* QUESTION
down: *see* FALL; WIN
downpour: *see* STORM
draft: *see* PLAN
draw: *see* PLAN
drawing: *see* PLAN
dread: *see* DANGER
drive: *see* CAMPAIGN
drop: *see* FALL
dubious: *see* QUESTION
due: *see* PREDICT
dupe: *see* STEAL
duplicity: *see* STEAL
duty: *see* TAX
dwindle: *see* FALL

E

eager: *see* ARDENT
eagerness: *see* ARDENT
earn: *see* GET
earthquake: *see* SHAKE
ease: *see* RELIEVE
ebb: *see* FALL
edict: *see* ORDER
edifice: *see* BUILDING
effort: *see* CAMPAIGN
elect: *see* CHOOSE
election: *see* CHOOSE
electrify: *see* PUZZLE
elope: *see* DISAPPEAR
elude: *see* ESCAPE
embezzle: *see* STEAL
embezzlement: *see* STEAL
emit: *see* GIVE
encourage: *see* APPROVAL
end: *see* RELIEVE; STOP
endanger: *see* DANGER
endorse: *see* APPROVAL
endorsement: *see* APPROVAL
endow: *see* GIVE
endowment: *see* GIVE
enemy: *see* OPPOSITION
enhance: *see* RISE
enjoin: *see* ORDER; STOP
enlarge: *see* RISE
enrage: *see* ANNOY
enter: *see* START
enterprise: *see* PLAN
enthusiasm: *see* ARDENT
enthusiastic: *see* ARDENT
entreat: *see* REQUEST
entreaty: *see* REQUEST
envisage: *see* PREDICT
erect: *see* BUILDING
ESCAPE: *see also* DISAPPEAR

Verbs

bolt
break
dodge
elude
evade
flee
get away
make off

Nouns

bolt
break

FALL (*cont.*)
narrow
pare
plunge
prune
recede
reduce
sag
shave
sink
slash
slump
trim
tumble
wane
Nouns
abatement
collapse
cut
decline
decrease
deflation
depression
descent
dive
drop
ebb
plunge
recede
reduction
slash
slump
Adverbs
down
low
off
fashion: *see* ORGANIZATION; PLAN
favor: *see* APPROVAL; BIAS
favoritism: *see* BIAS
fear: *see* DANGER
feel: *see* SAY
felicitate: *see* HONOR
felicitation: *see* HONOR
ferret: *see* DISCOVER
fervent: *see* ARDENT
fervor: *see* ARDENT
fete: *see* CEREMONY
fight: *see* OPPOSITION; VIOLENCE
filibuster: *see* STOP
final: *see* STOP
finale: *see* STOP
find: *see* DISCOVER; SAY
finish: *see* STOP
FIRE
Verbs
blaze
burn
flame
flare
ignite
Nouns
blaze
conflagration
flames
holocaust
firm: *see* CALM; ORGANIZATION
first: *see* START
fix: *see* PLAN
flame: *see* FIRE
flames: *see* FIRE
flare: *see* FIRE; RISE
flay *: *see* OPPOSITION
flee: *see* ESCAPE
fleece: *see* STEAL
flight: *see* ESCAPE
FLOOD
Verbs
cover
deluge
inundate
submerge
wash
Nouns
inundation
overflow
torrent
flout: *see* OPPOSITION
flurry: *see* DANGER
foe: *see* OPPOSITION
foil: *see* STOP
follow: *see* PURSUE
forbid: *see* STOP

forecast: *see* PREDICT
foresee: *see* PREDICT
forestall: *see* STOP
foretell: *see* PREDICT
form: *see* ORGANIZATION
forum: *see* DISCUSS; MEETING
found: *see* START
fracas: *see* VIOLENCE
frame: *see* PLAN
fraud: *see* STEAL
fray: *see* VIOLENCE
free: *see* ACQUIT; RELIEVE
freedom: *see* ACQUIT
freeze: *see* COLD
fret: *see* ANNOY
fright: *see* DANGER
frighten: *see* DANGER
frigid: *see* COLD
frown: *see* OPPOSITION
fruitless: *see* LOSE
frustrate: *see* STOP
frustration: *see* STOP
furor: *see* VIOLENCE
further: *see* APPROVAL
fury: *see* ANNOY; VIOLENCE
futile: *see* LOSE

G

gain: *see* RISE; GET
gainsay: *see* DENY
gale: *see* STORM
game: *see* OPPOSITION
gang: *see* ORGANIZATION
gather: *see* MEETING
gathering: *see* MEETING
GET: *see also* STEAL
Verbs
acquire
earn
gain
obtain
receive
win
Nouns
acquisition
getaway: *see* ESCAPE
gibe: *see* RIDICULE
gift: *see* GIVE
GIVE
Verbs
accord
afford
allocate
allot
apportion
bequeath
bestow
cede
confer
contribute
distribute
donate
emit
endow
grant
hand
issue
leave
offer
pay
present
provide
share
submit
vent
will
yield
Nouns
allocation
allotment
apportionment
award
bequest
bestowal
contribution
distribution
donation
endowment
gift
grant
legacy
offer

GIVE (*cont.*)
payment
present
provision
give in: *see* LOSE
give up: *see* LOSE
give way: *see* LOSE
go: *see* DISAPPEAR
gone: *see* DISAPPEAR
grant: *see* GIVE
gratify: *see* APPROVAL
GREET: *see also* CEREMONY
Verbs
cheer
hail
meet
receive
salute
welcome
Nouns
greeting
reception
welcome
greeting: *see* GREET
grip: *see* COLD; STORM
group: *see* ORGANIZATION
grow: *see* RISE
growth: *see* RISE
guard: *see* DANGER; HIDE
guide: *see* LEADER
guild: *see* ORGANIZATION
gut *: *see* DAMAGE

H

hail: *see* APPROVAL; GREET; HONOR
halt: *see* STOP
hand: *see* GIVE
harass: *see* ANNOY
harm: *see* DAMAGE
harmonize: *see* PEACE
harmony: *see* PEACE
harry: *see* ANNOY; PURSUE
hasten: *see* ADVANCE
hazard: *see* DANGER
head: *see* LEADER
heal: *see* PEACE
hearten: *see* APPROVAL
HEAT
Verbs
bake
oppress
sizzle
stifle
swelter
Nouns
mercury
temperature
thermometer
spell
wave
Adjectives
humid
oppressive
stifling
sultry
torrid
height: *see* PEAK
heighten: *see* RISE
help: *see* APPROVAL; RELIEVE
HIDE: *see also* ESCAPE
Verbs
bury
cache
cloak
conceal
guard
mask
screen
secrete
veil
withhold
Nouns
cache
cloak
mask
screen
veil
higher: *see* RISE
hinder: *see* STOP
hindrance: *see* STOP
hint: *see* SAY
hiss: *see* RIDICULE

hit: *see* ACCIDENT; OPPOSITION
hitch: *see* STOP
hold: *see* ARREST; CEREMONY; SAY
hold up: *see* STEAL; STOP
hold-up: *see* STEAL
holocaust: *see* FIRE
homage: *see* HONOR
homicide: *see* DEATH
HONOR: *see also* CEREMONY; GREET
Verbs
cheer
congratulate
eulogize
exalt
extol
felicitate
hail
lionize
revere
Nouns
congratulation
eulogy
felicitation
homage
reverence
tribute
hoot: *see* RIDICULE
hope: *see* PREDICT
hound: *see* PURSUE
house: *see* BUILDING; ORGANIZATION
howl: *see* STORM
humble: *see* WIN
humid: *see* HEAT
hunt: *see* PURSUE
hurricane: *see* STORM
hurt: *see* DAMAGE
hush: *see* CALM

I

icy: *see* COLD
idea: *see* PLAN
ignite: *see* FIRE
ignore: *see* BELITTLE
ill: *see* DIFFICULTY
imminent: *see* FACE
impair: *see* DAMAGE
impart: *see* SHOW
impede: *see* STOP
impel: *see* ADVANCE
impend: *see* FACE
imperil: *see* DANGER
impetus: *see* START
implicate: *see* ACCUSE
implore: *see* REQUEST
impose: *see* TAX
impost: *see* TAX
imprison: *see* STOP
improve: *see* RELIEVE
improvement: *see* RELIEVE
inaugurate: *see* START
inauguration: *see* START
inception: *see* START
increase: *see* RISE
indicate: *see* PREDICT; SHOW
indication: *see* PREDICT; SHOW
indict: *see* ACCUSE
indictment: *see* ACCUSE
indifference: *see* CALM
indifferent: *see* CALM
induct: *see* START
induction: *see* START
inertia: *see* CALM
inflate: *see* RISE
inflation: *see* RISE
influence: *see* LEADER
initial: *see* START
initiate: *see* START
injunction: *see* ORDER; STOP
injure: *see* DAMAGE
injury: *see* DAMAGE
inquire: *see* INVESTIGATE; QUESTION
inquiry: *see* INVESTIGATE; QUESTION
insist: *see* SAY
install: *see* START
installation: *see* START
institute: *see* MEETING; START
institution: *see* BUILDING; ORGANIZATION
intend: *see* PREDICT
intention: *see* PREDICT
interfere: *see* STOP
interference: *see* STOP

interrogate: *see* QUESTION
interrogation: *see* QUESTION
interrupt: *see* STOP
interruption: *see* STOP
intimate: *see* SAY
intimation: *see* SAY
inundate: *see* FLOOD
inundation: *see* FLOOD
INVESTIGATE
Verbs
analyze
delve
examine
inquire
plumb
probe *
pry *
scan
scrutinize
sift *
sound
study
Nouns
analysis
examination
inquiry
probe *
scrutiny
study
invitation: *see* REQUEST
invite: *see* REQUEST
invoke: *see* REQUEST
involve: *see* ACCUSE
irate: *see* ANNOY
ire: *see* ANNOY
irk: *see* ANNOY
irritate: *see* ANNOY
issue: *see* GIVE; POLICY; SHOW

J

jam: *see* STOP
jar: *see* SHAKE
jeer: *see* RIDICULE
jeopardize: *see* DANGER
jeopardy: *see* DANGER
jest: *see* RIDICULE
join: *see* ORGANIZATION
joke: *see* RIDICULE
jolt: *see* SHAKE
joy: *see* ARDENT
joyful: *see* ARDENT
jump: *see* RISE
justify: *see* APPROVAL

K

key: *see* DISCOVER
kidnap: *see* DISAPPEAR
kidnapping: *see* DISAPPEAR
kill: *see* DEATH
killing: *see* DEATH
knit: *see* ORGANIZATION

L

larceny: *see* STEAL
lash: *see* OPPOSITION; STORM
last: *see* STOP
latest: *see* STOP
laud: *see* APPROVAL
laugh: *see* RIDICULE
laughter: *see* RIDICULE
law: *see* ORDER
lay: *see* ACCUSE
lead: *see* DISCOVER; LEADER; WIN
LEADER
Verbs
command
control
dictate
direct
guide
head
influence
lead
persuade
reign
rule
sway
Nouns
authority
chairman
chief
command

LEADER (*cont.*)
commander
control
dictator
director
expert
head
notable
pioneer
president
regime
reign
rule
ruler
leaning: *see* BIAS
leave: *see* DISAPPEAR; GIVE; RESIGN
legacy: *see* GIVE
lessen: *see* FALL
let up: *see* RELIEVE
level: *see* DAMAGE
levy: *see* TAX
liable: *see* FACE
lift: *see* RELIEVE; RISE
lighten: *see* RELIEVE
likelihood: *see* PREDICT
likely: *see* PREDICT
liken: *see* COMPARE
likeness: *see* COMPARE
limit: *see* STOP
link: *see* ACCUSE; COMPARE; ORGANIZATION
lionize: *see* HONOR
list: *see* SHOW
load: *see* TAX
locality: *see* AREA
lock: *see* STOP
look for: *see* FACE
loom: *see* FACE
loosen: *see* RELIEVE
loot: *see* STEAL
LOSE: *see also* DISAPPEAR
Verbs
bow
fail
give in
give up
give way
submit
succumb
surrender
yield
Nouns
defeat
failure
loss
setback
surrender
Adjectives
fruitless
futile
vain
loss: *see* DAMAGE; DISAPPEAR; LOSE
low: *see* FALL

M

maintain: *see* SAY
make off: *see* ESCAPE
malady: *see* DIFFICULTY
malign: *see* BELITTLE
manslaughter: *see* DEATH
mantle: *see* SNOW
map: *see* PLAN
mar: *see* DAMAGE
mark: *see* CEREMONY
marshal: *see* MEETING
mask: *see* HIDE
master: *see* WIN
match: *see* OPPOSITION
measure: *see* ORDER
meet: *see* GREET; MEETING; REPLY
MEETING
Verbs
array
assemble
confer
congregate
convene
convoke
gather
marshal

MEETING (*cont.*)
meet
mobilize
rally
reunite
unite
Nouns
assemblage
assembly
conference
congress
convention
convocation
forum
gathering
institute
parley
rally
reunion
session
talk(s)
melee: *see* VIOLENCE
melt: *see* DISAPPEAR
menace: *see* DANGER
mercury: *see* COLD; HEAT
merge: *see* ORGANIZATION
merger: *see* ORGANIZATION
minimize: *see* BELITTLE
mishap: *see* ACCIDENT
missing: *see* DISAPPEAR
mitigate: *see* RELIEVE
mix-up: *see* VIOLENCE
mobilize: *see* MEETING
mock: *see* RIDICULE
mockery: *see* RIDICULE
modification: *see* REVISE
modify: *see* REVISE
mount: *see* RISE
move: *see* CAMPAIGN; START
muddle: *see* PUZZLE
mum *: *see* CALM
murder: *see* DEATH
mute: *see* CALM
mutiny: *see* VIOLENCE
mystery: *see* PUZZLE
mystify: *see* PUZZLE

N

name: *see* ACCUSE; CHOOSE; DESCRIBE
narrate: *see* DESCRIBE
narrative: *see* DESCRIBE
narrow: *see* FALL
near: *see* FACE
neighborhood: *see* AREA
net: *see* ARREST
neutral: *see* CALM
neutrality: *see* CALM
nip: *see* COLD
noise: *see* VIOLENCE
nominate: *see* CHOOSE
nomination: *see* CHOOSE
nonplus: *see* PUZZLE
notable: *see* LEADER
nullify: *see* OPPOSITION

O

oath: *see* PROMISE
observance: *see* CEREMONY
observe: *see* CEREMONY
obstacle: *see* STOP
obstruct: *see* STOP
obstruction: *see* STOP
obtain: *see* GET
off: *see* FALL
offer: *see* GIVE
onslaught: *see* OPPOSITION
onus: *see* DIFFICULTY
open: *see* START
opening: *see* START
opinion: *see* ORDER
oppose: *see* OPPOSITION
OPPOSITION: *see also* BELITTLE; STOP
Verbs
argue
assail
attack
ban
bar
battle
berate

OPPOSITION (*cont.*)

bicker
break
cancel
censure
challenge
chide
clash
combat
condemn
conflict
contest
debate
decry
defy
denounce
deplore
differ
disagree
disapprove
discard
dislike
dispute
dissent
divide
eschew
fight
flay *
flout
frown
hit *
lash
nullify
outlaw
pit *
protest
quarrel
rap
rebuff
rebuke
reject
repel
reproach
reprove
repudiate
rule out

OPPOSITION (*cont.*)

slap *
split
upbraid
veto
vie
void
war

Nouns

adversary
argument
assault
attack
battle
blow
breach
break
censure
challenge
clash
combat
condemnation
conflict
contest
controversy
defiance
denunciation
disapproval
discord
dislike
dispute
dissension
dissent
division
enemy
fight
foe
game
match
onslaught
protest
quarrel
rebuff
rebuke
reproach
rift

OPPOSITION (*cont.*)
rival
row
schism
split
strife
struggle
tilt *
tournament
tourney
war

oppress: *see* HEAT
oppressive: *see* HEAT

ORDER
Verbs
bid
charge
command
control
decree
dictate
direct
enjoin
prescribe
rule
tell
Nouns
act
award
command
control
decision
decree
dictation
edict
injunction
law
measure
opinion
ordinance
rule
ruling
statute
ukase *
verdict
writ

ordinance: *see* ORDER

ORGANIZATION
Verbs
absorb
ally
band
combine
consolidate
develop
fashion
form
join
knit
link
merge
pool
shape
tie
unite
weld
Nouns
alliance
association
band
board
body
bond
branch
center
club
combination
combine *
commission
committee
company
concern
corporation
corps
firm
gang
group
guild
house
institution
merger
party

ORGANIZATION (*cont.*)
pool
racket
ring
society
syndicate
tie
union
unit
organize: *see* ORGANIZATION
oust: *see* RESIGN
ouster: *see* RESIGN
outlaw: *see* OPPOSITION; STEAL
outline: *see* DESCRIBE; PLAN
outlook: *see* PREDICT
overcome: *see* WIN
overflow: *see* FLOOD
overwhelm: *see* WIN
own: *see* ADMIT

P

pacify: *see* PEACE
pact: *see* PEACE
pageant: *see* CEREMONY
panacea: *see* RELIEVE
panic: *see* VIOLENCE
parade: *see* CEREMONY
parallel: *see* COMPARE
paralyze: *see* STOP
pare: *see* FALL
parley: *see* MEETING
partial: *see* BIAS
party: *see* CEREMONY; ORGANIZATION
pass: *see* APPROVAL
passage: *see* APPROVAL
patch: *see* PEACE
pause: *see* STOP
pay: *see* GIVE
payment: *see* GIVE
PEACE
Verbs
agree
arbitrate
conciliate
harmonize
heal
pacify
patch
placate
reconcile
settle
smooth
Nouns
accord
agreement
amity
arbitration
armistice
arrangement
bargain
compact
conciliation
concord
deal
harmony
pact *
settlement
transaction
treaty
truce
PEAK
Verbs
cap
climax
crown
top
Nouns
acme
cap
climax
crest
crown
height
top
perceive: *see* PREDICT
perfect: *see* PLAN
perform: *see* CEREMONY
performance: *see* CEREMONY
peril: *see* DANGER
perish: *see* DEATH

permission: *see* APPROVAL
permit: *see* APPROVAL
perplex: *see* PUZZLE
persuade: *see* LEADER
pick: *see* CHOOSE
picture: *see* DESCRIBE
pigeonhole: *see* POSTPONE
pioneer: *see* LEADER
pit: *see* OPPOSITION
placate: *see* PEACE; RELIEVE
place: *see* AREA
PLAN
Verbs
agree
aim
arrange
conspire
decide
design
determine
draft
draw
expect
fashion
fix
frame
map
outline
perfect
plot
polish
prepare
project
propose
scheme
set
shape
sketch
suggest
Nouns
agenda
agreement
aim
arrangement
chart
conspiracy

PLAN (*cont.*)
design
drawing
enterprise
idea
outline
plot
program
project
proposal
scheme
sketch
suggestion
undertaking
plank: *see* POLICY
plant: *see* BUILDING
platform: *see* POLICY
plaudit: *see* APPROVAL
plea: *see* REQUEST
plead: *see* REQUEST
please: *see* APPROVAL
pledge: *see* PROMISE
plot: *see* PLAN
plumb: *see* INVESTIGATE
plunder: *see* STEAL
plunge: *see* FALL
poised: *see* FACE
POLICY
Nouns
attitude
belief
issue
plank
platform
stand
subject
topic
view
polish: *see* PLAN
pool: *see* ORGANIZATION
portray: *see* DESCRIBE
portrayal: *see* DESCRIBE
posse: *see* PURSUE
possibility: *see* PREDICT
possible: *see* PREDICT
POSTPONE: *see also* STOP

POSTPONE (*cont.*)
Verbs
defer
delay
pigeonhole
prolong
put off
shelve
table
Nouns
delay
postponement
postponement: *see* POSTPONE
pound: *see* STORM
pray: *see* REQUEST
prayer: *see* REQUEST
PREDICT: *see also* FACE
Verbs
anticipate
envisage
expect
forecast
foresee
foretell
hope
indicate
intend
perceive
prophesy
scent
schedule
see
slate
vision
warn
Nouns
anticipation
expectation
forecast
hope
indication
intention
likelihood
outlook
possibility
prediction

PREDICT (*cont.*)
probability
prophecy
vision
warning
Adjectives
due
likely
possible
probable
prediction: *see* PREDICT
prejudice: *see* BIAS
prepare: *see* FACE; PLAN
prescribe: *see* ORDER
present: *see* GIVE
president: *see* LEADER
press: *see* ADVANCE
prevail: *see* WIN
prevent: *see* STOP
primary: *see* START
probability: *see* PREDICT
probable: *see* PREDICT
probe *: *see* INVESTIGATE
procession: *see* CEREMONY
proclaim: *see* SAY
prod: *see* ADVANCE
program: *see* CAMPAIGN; PLAN
progress: *see* ADVANCE
prohibit: *see* STOP
prohibition: *see* STOP
project: *see* PLAN
prolong: *see* POSTPONE
PROMISE: *see also* PEACE
Verbs
agree
assure
pledge
swear
vow
Nouns
agreement
assurance
avowal
oath
pledge
vow

prophecy: *see* PREDICT
prophesy: *see* PREDICT
proposal: *see* PLAN
propose: *see* APPROVAL; PLAN
protect: *see* DANGER
protest: *see* OPPOSITION
provide: *see* GIVE
provision: *see* GIVE
prune: *see* FALL
pry *: *see* INVESTIGATE
publish: *see* SHOW
PURSUE
Verbs
chase
follow
harry
hound
hunt
search
seek
trace
track
trail
Nouns
chase
expedition
hunt
posse
pursuit
quarry
quest
search
trace
track
trail
pursuit: *see* PURSUE
push: *see* ADVANCE
put off: *see* POSTPONE
PUZZLE
Verbs
amaze
astonish
astound
awe
baffle
balk
PUZZLE (*cont.*)
bewilder
confound
confuse
electrify
mystify
nonplus
perplex
shock
stagger
startle
stun
surprise
Nouns
amazement
astonishment
awe
bewilderment
confusion
muddle
mystery
shock
snarl
surprise
tangle

Q

quake: *see* SHAKE
quarrel: *see* OPPOSITION
quarry: *see* PURSUE
quell: *see* STOP
query: *see* QUESTION
quest: *see* PURSUE
QUESTION: *see also* INVESTIGATE
Verbs
ask
catechize
challenge
doubt
inquire
interrogate
query
quiz *
Nouns
challenge
doubt

QUESTION (*cont.*)
inquiry
interrogation
query
Adjectives
doubtful
dubious
quicken: *see* ADVANCE
quiet: *see* CALM
quit: *see* DISAPPEAR; RESIGN
quiver: *see* SHAKE
quiz *: *see* QUESTION
quotation: *see* SAY
quote: *see* SAY

R

racket: *see* ORGANIZATION; STEAL
racketeer: *see* STEAL
rage: *see* ANNOY; STORM
raid: *see* STEAL
rally: *see* MEETING
ram: *see* ACCIDENT
ransack: *see* STEAL
rap *: *see* OPPOSITION
ratification: *see* APPROVAL
ratify: *see* APPROVAL
ravage: *see* DAMAGE
raze: *see* DAMAGE
ready: *see* FACE
realign: *see* REVISE
realignment: *see* REVISE
rear: *see* BUILDING
rebel: *see* VIOLENCE
rebellion: *see* VIOLENCE
rebuff: *see* OPPOSITION
rebuke: *see* OPPOSITION
rebuttal: *see* REPLY
recant: *see* DENY
recede: *see* FALL
receive: *see* GET; GREET; MEETING
reception: *see* GREET
reconcile: *see* PEACE
record: *see* SHOW
rectify: *see* RELIEVE
reduce: *see* FALL
reduction: *see* FALL
reform: *see* RELIEVE
refusal: *see* DENY
refuse: *see* DENY
refutation: *see* DENY; REPLY
refute: *see* DENY; REPLY
regard: *see* SAY
regime: *see* LEADER
region: *see* AREA
register: *see* SHOW
reign: *see* LEADER
reject: *see* DENY; OPPOSITION
rejection: *see* DENY
rejoinder: *see* REPLY
relate: *see* DESCRIBE
relax: *see* RELIEVE
release: *see* ACQUIT
relief: *see* RELIEVE
RELIEVE: *see also* APPROVAL
Verbs
abolish
aid
allay
alleviate
better
correct
cure
ease
end
free
help
improve
lift
lighten
loosen
mitigate
placate
rectify
reform
relax
remedy
repair
rescue
rid
save
slacken
soften

RELIEVE (*cont.*)
succor
temper
Nouns
abolition
aid
alleviation
betterment
correction
corrective
cure
end
help
improvement
let up
panacea
reform
relief
remedy
rescue
succor

remedy: *see* RELIEVE
renounce: *see* DENY
renunciation: *see* DENY
repair: *see* RELIEVE
repel: *see* OPPOSITION; STOP

REPLY: *see also* DENY
Verbs
answer
meet
refute
respond
retort
Nouns
answer
rebuttal
refutation
rejoinder
response
retort

report: *see* DESCRIBE
repress: *see* STOP
repression: *see* STOP
reproach: *see* OPPOSITION
reproof: *see* OPPOSITION
reprove: *see* OPPOSITION
repudiate: *see* DENY; OPPOSITION
repudiation: *see* DENY
repulse: *see* STOP; WIN
repulsion: *see* STOP

REQUEST: *see also* APPROVAL
Verbs
appeal
ask
beg
beseech
bid
call for
demand
desire
entreat
exhort
implore
invite
invoke
plead
pray
seek
solicit
urge
want
Nouns
appeal
demand
desire
entreaty
invitation
plea
prayer

rescue: *see* RELIEVE

RESIGN
Verbs
abandon
abdicate
depose
desert
dismiss
expel
leave
oust
quit
retire

RESIGN (*cont.*)
Nouns
abandonment
abdication
desertion
dismissal
expulsion
leave
ouster
resignation
retirement
resignation: *see* RESIGN
respond: *see* REPLY
response: *see* REPLY
restrain: *see* STOP
restraint: *see* STOP
restrict: *see* STOP
restriction: *see* STOP
result: *see* ADVANCE
retard: *see* STOP
retire: *see* RESIGN
retirement: *see* RESIGN
retort: *see* REPLY
retract: *see* DENY
retraction: *see* DENY
reunion: *see* MEETING
reunite: *see* MEETING
reveal: *see* SHOW
revelation: *see* SHOW
revenue: *see* TAX
revere: *see* HONOR
reverence: *see* HONOR
review: *see* CEREMONY
REVISE
Verbs
adjust
alter
amend
change
modify
realign
shake up
shift
switch
transfer
transform

REVISE (*cont.*)
vary
Nouns
adjustment
alteration
amendment
change
modification
realignment
revision
shake-up
shift
switch
transformation
variation
revision: *see* REVISE
revolt: *see* VIOLENCE
revolution: *see* VIOLENCE
rid: *see* RELIEVE
RIDICULE: *see also* OPPOSITION
Verbs
boo
chide
deride
gibe
hiss
hoot
insult
jeer
jest
joke
laugh
mock
scoff
scorn
scout
sneer
taunt
tease
twit
Nouns
boo
catcall
derision
gibe
hiss

RIDICULE (*cont.*)
hoot
insult
jeer
jest
joke
laughter
mockery
scorn
sneer
taunt
rifle: *see* STEAL
rift: *see* OPPOSITION
ring: *see* ORGANIZATION
riot: *see* VIOLENCE
RISE: *see also* BUILDING
Verbs
add
arise
ascend
augment
broaden
climb
develop
enhance
enlarge
exceed
expand
extend
flare
gain
grow
heighten
increase
inflate
jump
lift
mount
skyrocket
soar
surpass
swell
tower
wax
widen
Nouns

RISE (*cont.*)
addition
ascension
ascent
climb
expansion
extension
gain
growth
increase
inflation
jump
Adverbs
higher
up
risk: *see* DANGER
rival: *see* OPPOSITION
rob: *see* STEAL
robbery: *see* STEAL
rock: *see* SHAKE
round up: *see* ARREST
round-up: *see* ARREST
rout: *see* WIN
row: *see* OPPOSITION; VIOLENCE
ruin: *see* DAMAGE
rule: *see* SAY; LEADER; ORDER
rule out: *see* OPPOSITION
ruler: *see* LEADER
ruling: *see* ORDER
runaway: *see* DISAPPEAR; ESCAPE
ruse: *see* STEAL
rush: *see* ADVANCE

S

sag: *see* FALL
salute: *see* GREET
sanction: *see* APPROVAL
save: *see* RELIEVE
SAY
Verbs
address
affirm
allege
assert
aver *
avow

SAY (*cont.*)
believe
charge
chat
cite
claim *
consider
contend
decide
declare
deem
discern
explain
expound
feel
find
hint
hold
insist
intimate
maintain
proclaim
quote
regard
rule
see
speak
state *
suggest
swear
talk
tell
testify
think
utter
view
voice
Nouns
address
affirmation
allegation
assertion
avowal
belief
charge
chat

SAY (*cont.*)
claim
contention
declaration
explanation
hint
intimation
quotation
speech
statement
suggestion
talk
testimony
utterance
view

scan: *see* INVESTIGATE
scare *: *see* DANGER
scene: *see* AREA
scent: *see* DANGER; PREDICT
schedule: *see* PREDICT
scheme: *see* PLAN
schism: *see* OPPOSITION
scoff: *see* RIDICULE
score: *see* WIN
scorn: *see* RIDICULE
scout: *see* DENY; RIDICULE
screen: *see* HIDE
scrutinize: *see* INVESTIGATE
scrutiny: *see* INVESTIGATE
search: *see* PURSUE
secrete: *see* HIDE
section: *see* AREA
see: *see* PREDICT; SAY
seek: *see* APPROVAL; PURSUE; REQUEST
seize: *see* ARREST; STEAL
seizure: *see* ARREST
select: *see* CHOOSE
selection: *see* CHOOSE
service: *see* CEREMONY
session: *see* MEETING
set: *see* PLAN
setback: *see* LOSE
settle: *see* PEACE
settlement: *see* PEACE
set up: *see* START

SHAKE

Verbs

jar
jolt
quake
quiver
rock
shock
totter
tremble
upset

Nouns

earthquake
jar
jolt
quake
quiver
shock
temblor *
tremor
upset

shake up: *see* REVISE
shake-up: *see* REVISE
shape: *see* ORGANIZATION; PLAN
share: *see* GIVE
shave: *see* FALL
shelve: *see* POSTPONE
shift: *see* REVISE
shock: *see* PUZZLE; SHAKE

SHOW

Verbs

announce
bare
betray
demonstrate
disclose
display
divulge
evince
exhibit
experiment
expose
impart
indicate
issue
list

SHOW (*cont.*)

publish
record
register
reveal
sound
test
try
uncover
unfold

Nouns

announcement
demonstration
disclosure
display
evidence
exhibit
exhibition
experiment
exposé
exposition
indication
record
revelation
test
trial

shun: *see* BELITTLE
sift *: *see* INVESTIGATE
silence: *see* CALM
silent: *see* CALM
sink: *see* FALL
site: *see* AREA
sizzle: *see* HEAT
sketch: *see* PLAN
skyrocket: *see* RISE
skyscraper: *see* BUILDING
slacken: *see* RELIEVE; STOP
slap *: *see* OPPOSITION
slash: *see* FALL
slate: *see* PREDICT
slaughter: *see* DEATH
slay: *see* DEATH
slaying: *see* DEATH
slight: *see* BELITTLE
slow: *see* STOP
slump: *see* FALL

slur: *see* BELITTLE
smash: *see* ACCIDENT; STORM
smash-up: *see* ACCIDENT
smooth: *see* PEACE
snag: *see* STOP
snarl: *see* PUZZLE; STOP
sneer: *see* RIDICULE
SNOW: *see also* COLD; STORM
Verbs
blanket
bury
choke
cloak
clog
cover
fall
mantle
Nouns
blanket
blizzard
cloak
fall
mantle
storm
soar: *see* RISE
society: *see* ORGANIZATION
soften: *see* RELIEVE
solicit: *see* REQUEST
solution: *see* DISCOVER
solve: *see* DISCOVER
sound: *see* INVESTIGATE; SHOW
speak: *see* SAY
spectacle: *see* CEREMONY
speech: *see* SAY
speed: *see* ADVANCE
spell: *see* COLD; HEAT
sphere: *see* AREA
split: *see* OPPOSITION
spoil: *see* DAMAGE
spur: *see* ADVANCE
spurn: *see* BELITTLE
stage: *see* CEREMONY
stagger: *see* PUZZLE
stall: *see* STOP
stampede: *see* VIOLENCE
stand: *see* POLICY
START
Verbs
act
begin
commence
create
enter
found
inaugurate
induct
initiate
install
institute
move
open
set up
Nouns
beginning
creation
impetus
inauguration
inception
induction
installation
move
opening
Adjectives
first
initial
primary
startle: *see* PUZZLE
state: *see* SAY
statement: *see* SAY
statute: *see* ORDER
stay: *see* STOP
STEAL
Verbs
cheat
deceive
defalcate
defraud
dupe
embezzle
extort
fleece
get

STEAL (*cont.*)
hold up
loot
plunder
raid
ransack
rifle
rob
seize
swindle
take
trick
wrest
Nouns
bandit
booty
burglar
burglary
defalcation
duplicity
embezzlement
extortion
fraud
hold-up
larceny
loot
outlaw
plunder
racket
racketeer
raid
robbery
ruse
swindle
theft
thief
thug
trick
stem: *see* STOP
stifle: *see* HEAT
stifling: *see* HEAT
still: *see* CALM
stimulate: *see* ADVANCE
stir: *see* ADVANCE; ANNOY
STOP: *see also* OPPOSITION
Verbs

STOP (*cont.*)
abate
abolish
avert
avoid
balk
ban
bar
block
cease
check
choke
clog
close
complete
cow
cripple
curb
curtail
deadlock
deter
end
enjoin
fail
filibuster
finish
foil
forbid
forestall
frustrate
halt
hinder
impede
imprison
interfere
interrupt
jam
limit
lock
obstruct
paralyze
pause
prevent
prohibit
quell
repel

STOP (*cont.*)
repress
repulse
restrain
restrict
retard
slacken
slow
snag
snarl
stall
stay
stem
suppress
suspend
tangle
terminate
thwart
tie up

Nouns

abatement
abolition
ban
bar
barrier
check
closing
completion
curb
curtailment
deadlock
end
filibuster
finale
finish
halt
hindrance
hitch
injunction
interference
interruption
jam
limit
obstacle
obstruction
pause

STOP (*cont.*)
prohibition
repression
restraint
restriction
snag
snarl
stay
suppression
suspension
tangle
tie-up

Adjectives

complete
final
last
latest

STORM: *see also* COLD; DAMAGE; FLOOD; SNOW

Verbs

batter
break
buffet
grip
howl
lash
pound
rage
smash
strike
sweep
toss
whirl
whistle

Nouns

blizzard
bolt
cloud-burst
cyclone
deluge
downpour
gale
hurricane
tempest
tornado
twister

STORM (*cont.*)
wind
story: *see* DESCRIBE
strain: *see* TAX
strife: *see* OPPOSITION
strike: *see* ACCIDENT; STORM
structure: *see* BUILDING
struggle: *see* OPPOSITION; VIOLENCE
study: *see* INVESTIGATE
stun: *see* PUZZLE
style: *see* DESCRIBE
subdue: *see* WIN
subject: *see* POLICY
submerge: *see* FLOOD
submit: *see* GIVE; LOSE
succeed: *see* WIN
success: *see* WIN
succor: *see* RELIEVE
succumb: *see* DEATH; LOSE
suggest: *see* APPROVAL; PLAN; SAY
suggestion: *see* PLAN; SAY
suicide: *see* DEATH
sultry: *see* HEAT
support: *see* APPROVAL
suppress: *see* STOP
suppression: *see* STOP
surpass: *see* RISE
surprise: *see* PUZZLE
surrender: *see* LOSE
suspend: *see* STOP
suspension: *see* STOP
sustain: *see* APPROVAL
swamp: *see* WIN
sway: *see* LEADER
swear: *see* PROMISE; SAY
sweep: *see* COLD; STORM; WIN
swell: *see* RISE
swelter: *see* HEAT
swindle: *see* STEAL
switch: *see* REVISE
symposium: *see* DISCUSS
syndicate: *see* ORGANIZATION

T

table: *see* POSTPONE
take: *see* ARREST; STEAL
take up: *see* DISCUSS
tale: *see* DESCRIBE
talk: *see* SAY
talk(s): *see* MEETING
tangle: *see* PUZZLE; STOP
tariff: *see* TAX
taunt: *see* RIDICULE
TAX
Verbs
assess
burden
exact
impose
levy
strain
Nouns
assessment
burden
custom
duty
exaction
excise
impost
levy
load
revenue
tariff
toll
tease: *see* RIDICULE
tell: *see* DESCRIBE; ORDER; SAY
temblor *: *see* SHAKE
temper: *see* RELIEVE
temperature: *see* COLD; HEAT
tempest: *see* STORM
tenement: *see* BUILDING
tense: *see* DANGER
tension: *see* DANGER
term: *see* DESCRIBE
terminate: *see* STOP
terrify: *see* DANGER
terror: *see* DANGER
terrorize: *see* DANGER
test: *see* SHOW
testify: *see* SAY
testimony: *see* SAY
theft: *see* STEAL

thermometer: *see* COLD; HEAT
thief: *see* STEAL
think: *see* DANGER
threat: *see* DANGER
threaten: *see* DANGER
thug: *see* STEAL
thwart: *see* STOP
tie: *see* ORGANIZATION
tie up: *see* STOP
tie-up: *see* STOP
tilt *: *see* OPPOSITION
toll: *see* TAX
top: *see* PEAK; WIN
topic: *see* POLICY
torment: *see* ANNOY
tornado: *see* STORM
torpor: *see* CALM
torrent: *see* FLOOD
torrid: *see* HEAT
toss: *see* STORM
totter: *see* SHAKE
tournament: *see* OPPOSITION
tourney: *see* OPPOSITION
tower: *see* BUILDING; RISE
trace: *see* PURSUE
track: *see* PURSUE
tract: *see* AREA
tragedy: *see* ACCIDENT
trail: *see* PURSUE
transaction: *see* PEACE
transfer: *see* REVISE
transform: *see* REVISE
transformation: *see* REVISE
trap: *see* ARREST
treaty: *see* PEACE
tremble: *see* SHAKE
tremor: *see* SHAKE
trial: *see* SHOW
tribute: *see* HONOR
trick: *see* STEAL
trim: *see* FALL
triumph: *see* WIN
trouble: *see* DANGER; DIFFICULTY; VIOLENCE
truce: *see* PEACE
true bill: *see* ACCUSE
try: *see* SHOW
tumble: *see* FALL
tumult: *see* VIOLENCE
turmoil: *see* VIOLENCE
twister: *see* STORM
twit: *see* RIDICULE

U

ukase *: *see* ORDER
unconcern: *see* CALM
unconcerned: *see* CALM
uncover: *see* SHOW
undermine: *see* BELITTLE
undertaking: *see* PLAN
unearth: *see* DISCOVER
unfair: *see* BIAS
unfold: *see* SHOW
union: *see* ORGANIZATION
unit: *see* ORGANIZATION
unite: *see* MEETING; ORGANIZATION
unmoved: *see* CALM
unravel: *see* DISCOVER
up: *see* RISE
upbraid: *see* OPPOSITION
uphold: *see* ACQUIT; APPROVAL
uprising: *see* VIOLENCE
uproar: *see* VIOLENCE
upset: *see* SHAKE
urge: *see* APPROVAL; REQUEST
utter: *see* SAY
utterance: *see* SAY

V

vain: *see* LOSE
vanish: *see* DISAPPEAR
vanquish: *see* WIN
variation: *see* REVISE
vary: *see* REVISE
veil: *see* HIDE
vent: *see* GIVE
verdict: *see* ORDER
veto: *see* OPPOSITION
vex: *see* ANNOY
vicinity: *see* AREA
victor: *see* WIN
victory: *see* WIN

vie: *see* OPPOSITION
view: *see* POLICY; SAY
vindicate: *see* ACQUIT
vindication: *see* ACQUIT
VIOLENCE: *see also* OPPOSITION
Verbs
battle
brawl
clamor
clash
combat
demonstrate
fight
mutiny
rebel
revolt
riot
stampede
struggle
Nouns
battle
brawl
chaos
clamor
clash
combat
conflict
confusion
demonstration
din
discord
disorder
disturbance
fight
fracas
fray
fury
furor
melee
mix-up
mutiny
noise
panic
rebellion
revolt
riot

VIOLENCE (*cont.*)
row
stampede
struggle
trouble
tumult
turmoil
uprising
uproar
vision: *see* PREDICT
voice: *see* SAY
void: *see* OPPOSITION
vote: *see* APPROVAL
vow: *see* PROMISE

W

wait: *see* FACE
wane: *see* FALL
want: *see* APPROVAL; REQUEST
war: *see* OPPOSITION
warn: *see* DANGER; PREDICT
warning: *see* PREDICT
wary: *see* DANGER
wash: *see* FLOOD
wave: *see* COLD; HEAT
wax: *see* RISE
weigh: *see* DISCUSS
welcome: *see* GREET
weld: *see* ORGANIZATION
whirl: *see* STORM
whistle: *see* STORM
widen: *see* RISE
will: *see* GIVE
WIN: *see also* GET
Verbs
beat
best
better
conquer
crush
defeat
down
excel
gain
humble
lead

WIN (*cont.*)
master
overcome
overwhelm
prevail
repulse
rout
score
subdue
succeed
swamp
sweep
top
triumph
vanquish
Nouns
lead
master
rout
success
sweep
triumph

WIN (*cont.*)
victor
victory

wind: *see* STORM
wintry: *see* COLD
withhold: *see* DENY; HIDE
woe: *see* DIFFICULTY
wrath: *see* ANNOY
wreck: *see* ACCIDENT; DAMAGE
wreckage: *see* DAMAGE
wrest: *see* STEAL
writ: *see* ORDER
wroth: *see* ANNOY

Y

yield: *see* GIVE; LOSE

Z

zeal: *see* ARDENT
zealous: *see* ARDENT
zone: *see* AREA

A GLOSSARY OF NEWSPAPER TERMS

AD Abbreviation for advertisement; referring usually to display advertisements. *See also* Add.

ADD Additional news matter; matter to be added to a news story. Frequently abbreviated to "ad."

AGATE Type 5½ points in depth. Agate lines are used to measure the length of newspaper columns and the depth of advertisements.

ANGLE A division or phase of a news story.

ASSIGNMENT A reporter's allotted task.

ASSIGNMENT MAN A reporter available for general work, as distinguished from one who has a fixed post.

BANK Part of a headline; a table on which type is kept after it has been set.

BANNER LINE A single-line headline in large type extending across the first page.

BEAT A reporter's fixed post, such as the City Hall beat; a story printed exclusively by one newspaper.

BINDER LINE A single line of large type, used on an inside page, under which is printed an unusually long story or a series of stories referring to a general subject.

BODY TYPE The type in which most of the newspaper is set; generally 8 point.

BOX Type framed by rules to give a box effect so that the type is more prominently displayed.

BREAK The point at which a story turns from the first page to an inside page, or from one column to another.

BULLDOG An early edition, usually of an afternoon newspaper.

BULLETIN Last-minute important news.

BUREAU A subsidiary news-gathering organization set up in an important center, such as Washington.

BY-LINE The reporter's signature preceding a story.

CANNED COPY Written information sent to the newspaper by the publicity bureaus of organizations, or by press agents.

CAPS Abbreviation for capitals.

CAPTION The explanatory lines above or below a newspaper photograph, illustration or diagram.

C.G.O. Means "Can go over" and designates stories of a character that permits them to be used at any time.

CHASE The metal frame in which the newspaper type is placed prior to the making of matrices and stereotype plates.

CHECK UP To investigate; to ascertain the truth or falsity of information.

CITY ROOM The place where the news organization functions.

CLIPS Abbreviation for clippings; refers to the stories clipped from the newspaper and preserved, concerning persons and events.

COMPOSITOR The typesetter.

COPY News manuscript.

COPY CUTTER The composing room employe who cuts the news manuscript into lengths or takes convenient for setting quickly and who has charge of the distribution of copy among the compositors.

COPYREADER Same as copy editor; the editor who puts the copy in its final shape before it is set and who writes the headlines.

COVER To obtain the facts of a news story.

CREDIT LINE The line that designates, if necessary, the source of a story or cut. "By the Associated Press" preceding a story is a credit line.

CROSSLINE Part of a headline distinguished from the top and the banks.

CUT Any newspaper photograph, illustration or diagram; also to reduce the length of a news story.

DATE LINE The name of the city or town and the date, which are placed at the beginning of stories not of local origin.

DAY SIDE That part of the newspaper organization that functions in the daytime.

DEAD News matter, particularly type, that has been eliminated and is no longer available for use.

DEADLINE The minute at which an edition of the newspaper must go to press.

DESK The copy desk at which news copy is edited and headlined.

DISTRICT MAN A reporter assigned to a specified district.

DOPE STORY A story, usually written under a by-line, that describes a situation and gives opinions of others as well as of the writer concerning the situation. Many political stories are "dope" stories.

DUPE Abbreviation for duplicate; if two stories giving the same facts inadvertently are printed in the same issue of the newspaper, one is a dupe. Dupe also designates the carbon copies of a story.

EARS Small boxes printed at each side of the title plate on the first page; they usually contain the weather forecast, the newspaper's slogan, circulation figures or like information.

EM A printer's measurement of type width.

EN Half an em.

EXCLUSIVE A story that is printed solely by one newspaper; a "beat" or a "scoop."

FEATURE A story that is timely and interesting but is not, strictly, news. To feature is to display prominently.

FILE To send a story by telegraph or cable.

FILLER Any matter that has no time restrictions and can be used when needed. Same as C.G.O.

FLAG The title plate of the newspaper on the first page.

FLASH A bulletin that gives the first brief information of an important event.

FLIMSY The carbon copies of news manuscript, which usually are tissue paper.

FLUSH Even with the column margin on either left or right side; no indentation as for a paragraph. "Flush and indent" is a direction to the compositor to set the first line of a piece of copy without indentation and to indent the succeeding lines at the left side. Same as hanging indentation.

FOLIO A page or a page number.

FOLLOW Sometimes used to designate a second-day news story; that is, a story developing from another, the facts of which have been printed.

FOLLOW COPY Direction to the compositor to set the copy exactly as it is written.

FOLO Abbreviation for follow. A follow story also is one that is subsidiary, but related to another.

FONT A complete set of type of one size and style.

FORM A complete page of type.

FUTURE A record of an event that is to take place.

GALLEY A metal tray to hold type.

GOOD NIGHT The closing of the news department after the final edition; to "get good night" is to be released from duty.

HEAD Abbreviation for headline.

HOLD FOR RELEASE Designation placed on copy that is to be set, but is not to be used until the direction to do so is given by the editor in charge.

HOLDING Holding the paper is putting back the edition deadline to wait for an important news story.

HTK, HTC Abbreviation for "head to come"; the designation placed on the first page of a story rushed to the composing room in takes, to indicate that the headline will follow.

INDENT *see* Flush

INSERT News matter to be incorporated in a story that has already been sent to the composing room and set in type. The copy of this matter is designated "insert."

JUMP The continuation of a first-page story on an inside page.

JUMP HEAD The headline that identifies the continuation of a first-page story.

KILL To eliminate from copy; to discard type as useless.

LABEL A headline that has no life or force, or a mere caption.

LATE WATCH After the rush of editing and printing the newspaper is over and most of the staff has gone off duty, a skeletonized staff remains to handle late stories and late editions. On a morning newspaper, the hours from 1 o'clock to 4 are the late watch.

LAYOUT A sheet, ruled into columns, indicating where the stories or the stories and advertisements will be placed in the newspaper page.

LEAD The introduction of a news story (pronounced leed).

LEAD Thin metal strips that are one, two and three points thick, used to space out lines of type. Also the process of spacing out type (pronounced led).

LEG MAN A reporter who gathers facts but does not write them.

LOBSTER SHIFT Same as Late Watch, or early watch on an afternoon paper.

MAKE OVER The process of rearranging a page of type, or a series of pages, to improve the appearance or to place new stories.

MAKE-UP The process of placing news stories and advertisements in the newspaper page.

MASTHEAD The heading on the editorial page that gives information about the newspaper.

MAT Abbreviation for matrix; the *papier-mâché* impression of a page of type from which a stereotype plate is made.

MINION Seven-point type.

MORGUE The place where newspaper clippings are filed.

MUST A designation placed on copy to indicate that it must be printed.

NIGHT SIDE That part of the newspaper staff that functions at night.

NONPAREIL Six-point type. It is also a unit of measurement for type widths, as the agate line is the measurement for depth.

OBIT Abbreviation for obituary; it means biographical material in general, not merely that of dead persons.

PAGE OPP Abbreviation for "page opposite," and means the page opposite the editorial page.

PICA Twelve-point type.

PICKUP Type already set that is to be incorporated into new matter; also the direction to the composing room to incorporate such type with new material being set.

PIED Pied type is type that is disarranged or jumbled so that it cannot be used.

PLEASE USE Similar to "must," but indicates only that it is desirable to use the story so marked.

POINT A point is 1/72 of an inch and is the unit of measurement for type sizes.

POSTSCRIPT A page made over between editions for imperative corrections or for important stories.

PRINTERS Composing-room employes who correct type and place it in the chases under the direction of make-up editors.

PROOF An impression of type on paper, on which corrections and other alterations are made.

PROOFREADER A composing room employe who checks the proof against the copy to detect errors made in typesetting.

PUT TO BED Closing the forms for an edition.

Q & A MATTER Abbreviation for "question and answer" matter. Testimony frequently is printed verbatim.

QUERY A telegraphic summary of a story sent by a correspondent, stating the number of words available. The telegraph editor judges the story by the summary, and orders the number of words required.

RAILROAD To rush copy to the composing room without close editing. This is resorted to only in emergencies.

RELEASE The order to print a story that has been set earlier and held to await instructions from an editor in charge. Also refers to "canned copy."

REPLATE Same as Postscript.

REPRINT Matter printed in late editions that has not reached readers of the early editions, and therefore is available for use in those editions in the following issue.

REWRITE To write for a second time to strengthen the story or to reduce it in length.

REWRITE MAN The reporter who takes the facts of stories over the telephone, assembles them and writes the story; he also revises copy written by other reporters to improve it or to cut it.

RIM The outer edge of the copy desk at which the copy editors sit.

ROTO Abbreviation for rotogravure.

RULE A metal strip, of the height of the type, that prints as a line. The printed line between the columns of a newspaper is made by a column rule.

RUN IN To incorporate into one paragraph a series of paragraphs or a list of names.

RUNNING STORY A story that is sent to the composing room from the copy desk in a series of short sections; *also* a continuing news story.

RUSH Designation placed on copy to insure speed in handling in the composing room.

SACRED COW Slang for a subject or story in which the publisher or higher editors are interested and which must be printed.

SCHEDULE The city editor's record of assignments; the copy editor's record of the stories he has edited and headlined.

SCOOP *See* Beat and Exclusive.

SECOND DAY *See* Follow

SECOND FRONT The first page of the second section of the newspaper; sometimes called the split page.

SEE COPY Direction from the copy desk to the composing room to verify a part of a story by reference to the copy. "Out see copy" means that a line or lines have been dropped and the copy must be referred to so that they may be restored.

SET AND HOLD *See* Hold for Release.

SHEET Slang for newspaper.

SHORTS Minor, brief stories.

SKELETONIZE The process of dropping words from cable copy so that the tolls will be reduced. Skeletonizing employs some code words, but the main saving is on articles and other words that may be eliminated without causing confusion to the copy desk in the home office.

SLOT Where the head of the copy desk sits.

SLUG The word or words placed on copy to designate the story. Also a piece of type metal.

SPIKE To spike is to discard copy by placing it on a spike.

SPLIT PAGE Same as Second Front.

SPREAD A lead story and all its subsidiary stories constitute a spread; also a story that requires a "top head," that is, one that goes at the top of a column; also sometimes used to designate the head itself.

STAR EDITION A one-star edition is the first; two-star the second; four or five-star is usually the final.

STET Let it stand; restore.

STICK The unit of measuring quantities of type. A stick is two inches of type.

STONE The bench or table, whose top is stone or metal, on which the pages lie in the composing room while they are made up.

SUBHEAD A line of prominent type in the body of a story to break up a long stretch of type and to indicate the subject matter of the type that appears under it.

SUMMARY A synopsis of a news story.

SYNDICATE An organization either connected with or separate from the newspaper that buys and sells news stories, features and other matter used by newspapers.

TABLE General term for any tabulated matter.

TAKE A section of a running story.

TIP Information from within or without the newspaper organization concerning a news event.

TRIM To reduce the length of a story; similar to Cut.

TURN RULE A rule has a broad edge and a fine edge. The ordinary position of the metal strip is with the fine edge up; but on the order "turn rule," the broad edge is turned up and is easily seen by the printer. It indicates to him that some correction or alteration is to be made at that place in the type.

TYPO Abbreviation for typographical error.

WHEN ROOM Same as C.G.O.

INDEX